Writing Accelerator

パラグラフ**構成要素**から**学べる**ライティング入門

SHOHAKUSHA

はしがき

　Writing Accelerator は日本人大学生のライティングスキルを無理なく伸ばすための教科書です。その名の通り、ややもすればしきいが高く感じられがちな「パラグラフ・ライティング」を facilitate（易しく）してくれる強力な「支援者」です。

本書の特長

▶▶ パラグラフ構成要素の丁寧な取り扱い

　用語としてのパラグラフ・ライティングはもはや高校生にさえ目新しいものではありません。しかし、よい導入文の特徴、よいトピックセンテンスの書き方、よい結論文の類型、などの細かい点は充分理解されているとは言えません。本書では、個別要素のひな型を具体的に明示することで、望ましいパラグラフが初心者にも必ず書けるような仕組みになっています。

▶▶ プロセスとしてのライティングの重視

　ライティングとは、既に心内に存在する「意味」を単に言語化して表現するだけの行為ではなく、それによって「意味」を整理し、また内容を深化させるような cyclical process（繰り返しのプロセス）です。本書では、Process of Paragraph Writing の項を設け、実際に brain storming で生み出されたアイデアの断片が、どのようなプロセスを経てパラグラフに仕上がるかを実況中継的に提示しています。

▶▶ 身近なトピックからグローバルイッシューまで

　ライティングとは、和文英訳のような第三者から与えられた意味を英語で置き換える作業ではなく、自ら表明したい意思を表現する営みです。日本の大学生に書くのにふさわしい内容があるはずです。本書は「好きな街」「今ハマっていること」などの取り組みやすい here-and-now で身近な話題から入り、最終的には「ジェンダーギャップ」「地球温暖化の影響」などの 21 世紀に生きる地球市民として誰もが直視すべき global issues を扱います。現代の大学生として「書きたくなる題材」と「書くにふさわしい題材」のバランスを重視しました。

▶▶ 他技能との有機的関連の重視

　ライティングの授業はともすれば個人個人でひたすら書くような単調な授業になりがちです。しかし書いたことは誰かに話したくなるのが当然ですし、逆に聞いたり話したりした経験が書く材料になることもしばしばです。本書は、Talking in Pairs というセクションを設け、書く（あるいは書いた）内容に関連してクラスメートとオーラル・コミュニケーションを行なう機会を出来る限り豊富に設定しています。

　インターネットやパソコンの普及に伴い、現在ライティングはキーボードを入力装置として行なうことが一般的になっています。キーボードライティングをも視野に入れたとき、従来は必要なかったような指導事項が必要になります。ひとつは全角文字と半角文字の関係、もうひとつは punctuation mark と spacing の問題です。本書では従来ほとんど触れられることのなかったこれらの点について丁寧な解説を加え、練習問題を設定しています。

>> 日本的事象に関する、また図やグラフにもとづく発信

　日本人の大学生が将来表現することを求められる可能性の高いトピックのひとつに日本的事象があります。自国の衣食住、生活習慣などについて表現できるようになっておくことはグローバルコミュニティの中でますます重要性が増すでしょう。本書では Unit 10 を日本的事象の表現練習にあて、日本の文化、風習などについて簡単に説明できる能力を養います。また Unit 12 ではグラフ、図など視覚情報をもとにしてパラグラフを書く練習をします。いわゆる information transfer の一種でもありますが、将来英語で論文を書くための、基礎訓練にもなります。

>> Focus on Form の重視

　ライティング上達のひとつの鍵はコミュニケーションとしてとにかく大量に書くことです。しかしそれだけでは効率が悪いことが知られており、折にふれ言語形式に意識的に注意を向けることが言語習得には必要と言われています。本書では Focusing on Form として、センテンスレベルの様々なトラブルスポットを取り上げ、editing の練習をする機会を豊富に提供しています。取り上げた英文はすべて大学生が実際に書いたものにもとづいていますので、非常に実用的な editing 練習をすることができます。

◆ まとめ

　本書は、日本人の大学生が、

1　書きたくなる、あるいは書くにふさわしいような話題について、
2　聞いたり話したり、という口頭コミュニケーション活動も行ないながら、
3　クラスメートとアドバイスを交換しながら、
4　英語的なパラグラフとして表現する練習をする

ためのまったく新しいタイプの process writing の教科書です。

　この Writing Accelerator を使って学習するみなさんが、自分の意図を読み手に効果的に伝える力をつけてくれることを祈っています。

2023 年秋

靜　哲人

Contents

Photo and illustration Acknowledgments

p. 1:（右・左）© sasadai ／ p. 2:（上段左）©
Thx4Stock;（上段右）© 89stocker;（下段左）©
Rita_Kochmarjova;（下段中）© drone.studio;
（下段右）© PR Image Factory ／ p. 9:（左）©
Tada Images;（右）© Andrey_Popov ／ p. 16:
（左）© Amnaj Khetsamtip;（右上）© RYUSHI;
（右下）© metamorworks ／ p. 21:（左上）©
Microgen;（右下）© panitanphoto ／ p. 35 :
© Nejron Photo ／ p. 36:（上段左）© kuremo;
（下段左）© picture cells;（中）© kuremo ;（上
段右）© Takamex;（下段右）© picture cells
／ p. 45:（上段左）© Popel Arseniy;（上段
中）© yarayanastia;（上段右）© Lordn;（下
段左）© SeventyFour;（下段中）© Rawpixel.
com;（下段右）© DavidTB ／ p. 53:（上段左）
© Horth Rasur;（上段中）© milatas;（上段右）
© KPG-Payless;（下段左から）© west_photo;
© mTaira;© yamasan0708;© buritora ／ p. 61:
（左上）© sulit.photos;（左）© maruco;（中）©
oatawa;（右）© BearFotos ／ p. 68:（上段左）
© beeboys;（上段右）© Princess_Anmitsu;（下
段左）© west_photo;（下段中）© TimeImage
Production;（下段右）© Taro_since2017; ／
p. 77:（上段左）© Rei Imagine;（上段中）©
Dpongvit;（上段右）© Citta Studio;（下段
左）© AaronChenPS2;（下段中）© Andriy
Blokhin;（下段右上）© Benoist / okimo;（下
段右上）© TOMO ／ p. 84:（上段左）© Vadim
Zakharishchev;（上段中）© Nor Gal;（上段右）
© Lukas Gojda;（下段左）© Cowen Duggar;
（下段右）© Infinity T29 ／ p. 93:（上段左）©
astudio;（上段右）© Pressmaster;（下段左）©
takayuki;（下段中）© JoeyCheung;（下段右）©
StevenK

Stage 1

Learning About a Paragraph

UNIT

1

A Paragraph as a Product
パラグラフは「段落」じゃない

言語にはそれぞれ固有の論理展開があります。この Unit では英語の論理展開の基本的パタンを学習しましょう。

複数のセンテンスがまとまってひとつのアイデアを表現しているものをパラグラフ (paragraph) と呼びます。パラグラフは次のような形をしています。

Why Singing English Songs Improves Your Pronunciation

Singing English songs is a good way to improve your English pronunciation. First, singing your favorite songs will lead to pronouncing the same words and phrases many times. You will learn to pronounce them smoothly. Second, singing songs provides many opportunities to practice natural, connected speech. Songs are full of linking, deletion, and other sound changes. Third, singing helps you to get your syllables correct. Singing English songs, you will learn not to insert unnecessary vowels like many Japanese learners of English do. Therefore, if you want to make your pronunciation better, you should practice singing in English.

コラム：音節 (syllable) と音符の関係

　音節とは、原則として母音を中心とする音のカタマリのことです。例えば second を辞書で引くと sec-ond のように "-" で区切って表記されています。これはこの語が sec と ond というふたつの音節で出来ていることを表します。日本語ネイティブは単語の最後で、d だけを発音するのが苦手なため、おうおうにして「secon ド」(=secondo) のように発音してしまいます。そういう発音だと最後の母音 o の分だけ、音節の数が増えたことになります。

　一方、歌の場合、メロディの音符の数と歌詞の音節の数が基本的には一致します。つまり、音節が 2 つの単語である second を歌詞に使うときには、メロディの音符も 2 つだけです。よって日本語カタカナ式に、secondo のような音節数を 3 つに増やした発音をしていると、メロディに合わせて歌えないことになります。メロディに合わせようとするとどうしても音節数を正しくせざるを得ません。

Task 1-1

上のパラグラフの中で、
(1) 全体の内容をまとめて書いているセンテンスはいくつありますか。そのようなセンテンスに下線を引きましょう。
(2) (1)で下線を引いたセンテンスが述べている内容の根拠は、大きく分けていくつ挙げられていますか。それぞれの根拠を述べる部分が始まる最初の語に○をつけましょう。

Task 1-2

上のパラグラフの最初と最後のセンテンスの関係は、次のうちどれですか。
A. The two sentences are exactly the same; saying the same thing using the same

wording.

B. The two sentences are saying two different things; the latter introduces a new topic.

C. The two sentences are saying almost the same thing using slightly different words.

Task 1-3

次の用語について音声もしくは先生の説明を聞き、要点をメモしましょう。

»» indentation
🔊 Audio 02

»» topic sentence
🔊 Audio 03

»» supporting sentences
🔊 Audio 04

»» concluding sentence
🔊 Audio 05

Task 1-4

p. 3 のパラグラフの ...

（1）indentation が起こっている部分にチェックをつけ、

（2）topic sentence の最初に TS と書き、

（3）それぞれの major point が始まるセンテンスの最初に、MP1 , MP2 , ... と書き、

（4）concluding sentence の最初に CS と書きましょう。

NOTE: concluding sentence を持たないパラグラフも現実には多くありますが、本書では、最も基本となるフォーマットを繰り返し練習するという意味で、パラグラフには topic sentence とともに、必ず concluding sentence をつけることにします。

Task 1-5

📶 Audio 06

パラグラフは一見、日本語の文章の「段落」の英語版のようですが、その構成は大きく違います。音声あるいは先生の説明を聞き、要点をメモしましょう。

an English paragraph	a Japanese *danraku*

Task 1-6

次の A, B では、どちらが英語らしいパラグラフか選びましょう。

A   I believe that, for classes of 100 or more students, lectures should be provided via video on demand. There is little point in insisting on face-to-face instruction in a large class. This is because in such a class there can be little interaction between the professor and the students. From the students' perspective, listening to a one-way lecture is virtually the same as watching a video recording. In fact, recorded lectures have many advantages over face-to-face lectures. They can be viewed at a convenient time, in a convenient place, and in a convenient manner.

B   Some classes in university are very large. Some have more than 100 students. In such a class there can be little interaction between the professor and the students. From the students' perspective, listening to a one-way lecture is virtually the same as watching a video recording. In fact, recorded lectures have many advantages over face-to-face lectures. They can be viewed at a convenient time, in a convenient place, and in a convenient manner. There is little point in insisting on face-to-face instruction in a large class. Therefore, I believe that, for classes of 100 or more students, lectures should be provided via video on demand.

Task 1-7   🔊 Audio 07

次のセンテンスが英語らしいパラグラフを構成するためには、どのような順番が最も適切か考えましょう。解答は音声を聞いて確認しましょう。

A) Dogs that do not get to spend time with their parents are more likely to develop behavior problems later on.
B) This problem could be solved if pet stores were not allowed to sell puppies under 6 months old.
C) People who buy dogs at pet stores tend to want little, cute ones.
D) I suggest that Japan should ban pet stores from selling puppies under 6 months old.
E) Owners who buy a dog because it is cute will abandon it as soon as it starts behaving in a problematic manner.
F) Thus, more and more dogs are abandoned and eventually killed.
G) To meet that demand, little puppies that should still be with their parents are separated from them.

🖥 Focusing on Form

Zenkaku Characters vs. *Hankaku* Characters

PC のキーボードに慣れていない人がタイプした英語は、つぎのような外観になることがあります。

T o d a y , u n i v e r s i t i e s c a n o f f e r c l a s s e s i n
a t l e a s t t h r e e d i f f e r e n t w a y s . C l a s s e s c a n
b e g i v e n f a c e - t o - f a c e , o n l i n e , o r v i a o n - d e
m a n d v i d e o s . E a c h s t y l e h a s i t s s t r e n g t h s
a n d w e a k n e s s e s .

これは日本語のフォントの「全角文字」で打った英文字です。見かけは英語のようですが、実はコンピュータは英語と認識してくれません。例えばマウスで選択して別の英語フォントに変えようと思っても変わりません。この「英文」を日本語フォントのないパソコンに送信すると文字化けしてしまいます。また、妙に横に間延びして、しかも行の右端を見ると単語の途中のあらぬところ（音節の切れ目以外の場所）で改行されてしまうことがあります。このような英語を打たないようにしましょう。

英語は英語のフォント（Times New Roman とか Century など）を使って「半角文字」（1 バイト文字とも言う）で打つ必要があり、正しくは次のような外観になります。

Today universities can offer classes in at least three different ways. Classes can be given face-to-face, online, or via on-demand video. Each style has its strengths and weaknesses.

これに関連して、以下の点も覚えておいてください。

☑ 行の一番右にいっても改行記号を入れ（つまり、リターンキーを押し）てはいけません。
　改行はパソコンが自動的にしてくれます。自分で改行記号を入れてよいのはパラグラフの最後だけです。

☑ 単語が行の切れ目にかかりそうになると、パソコンが自動的にその語全体を次の行に送ってくれます。よってパソコンで打っている時は、わざわざ自分でハイフンを入れて単語の途中で改行する必要はありません。

☑ 手書きの場合にも、ハイフンを入れる正しい位置（音節の切れ目）を辞書なしで知るのは至難の技です。よって、どんな場合にも語の途中では改行せず、行の右端が多少デコボコになっても、単語ごと次行から始めるのがもっとも安全で確実な方法です。

Writing a Topic Sentence
主題文で要点を宣言

この Unit では topic sentence についてさらに深く学び、
良い topic sentence を書く練習をします。

Unit 1 では、topic sentence については、およそ次のような説明がなされました。

The topic sentence of a paragraph presents the main idea of the paragraph.

Task 2-1

Audio 08

音声を聞き、
(1) main idea に必要な２つの要素をメモしましょう。
(2) A〜Fが、topic sentence として良いか悪いかチェックしましょう。

a main idea = [   ] + [   ]

A) I am going to write about how I spend my free time.   [   ]
B) The topic of my paragraph is YouTube.   [   ]
C) I spend my free time mostly by watching YouTube.   [   ]
D) My favorite way of spending free time is watching YouTube.   [   ]
E) I usually spend my free time watching my favorite channels on YouTube.
                                                                [   ]
F) How do you spend your free time?   [   ]

Task 2-2

1.〜4. のパラグラフには topic sentence がありません。topic sentence として最も適当なものをそれぞれ A〜C から選びましょう。自分の答えが決まったらクラスメートと確認してみましょう。

1. _____ First, the operating systems are different. Macs use macOS while PCs use Windows. Second, Macs have a comparatively smaller range of software while PCs have all kinds of software. Third, Macs are generally more expensive than PCs with similar specifications.

A) The number of Mac users worldwide is much smaller than that of Windows users.

B) Macs and PCs are both computers, but there are several differences between them.

C) I believe Macs are more suitable to be used for a hobby than for work.

2. _____ Firstly, what kind of work are you passionate about? Make a list of activities you like and spend time on. Second, know your strengths. It will be much easier if you have a job in which you can do what you are good at. Third, know your personality. Depending on your personality, there are different career paths that will suit you.

A) It is undeniable that some jobs are better paid than other jobs.
B) No doubt you are wondering what kind of career to choose when you graduate.
C) There are a number of things to consider when choosing a career.

3. _____ Firstly, you can buy e-books much more quickly. When you click on a book, it downloads to your device in an instant. Secondly, e-books are generally cheaper than paper books. Thirdly, they can be stored easily on an electronic device such as your mobile phone, making them more portable.

A) E-books have several advantages over paper books.
B) E-books have changed our traditional definition of what a book is.
C) E-books have strengths and weaknesses compared to paper books.

4. _____ The main advantage is that you can watch the video at a time and pace that is convenient for you. You can decide when you want to watch it and how fast or slow you want to watch it. You can double the speed or rewind it as many times as you want. Another advantage is that you don't have to go to the university to watch it. You can watch it at home. A disadvantage is that it is easy to forget to watch it. As no one manages the time for you, you have to be strong-willed to stick to your schedule. It can also be a lonely task because there is no interaction between you and the professor or between you and your classmates.

A) Using on-demand video as a teaching tool only benefits teachers.
B) On-demand video lessons cannot be called lessons.
C) Watching on-demand videos as a class has both advantages and disadvantages.

1. ～ 3. のパラグラフには topic sentence がありません。supporting sentences をよく
読んで、適当な topic sentence の例を書いてみましょう。

1. _____ The Student Survey is
conducted at the end of each semester. Students take about 15 minutes to
say what they think of each course they have taken. The university says
that the results are carefully analyzed by the Class Survey Committee and
reported to all teachers at the Faculty Meeting. Unfortunately, nothing seems
to change. Boring classes remain boring and unreasonable teachers remain
unreasonable. I do not think the survey is worth our precious time.

2. _____ The Student Survey is
conducted at the end of each semester. Students take about 15 minutes to
say what they think of each course they have taken. The university says
that the results are carefully analyzed by the Class Survey Committee and
reported to all teachers at the Faculty Meeting. Unfortunately, nothing
seems to change. Perhaps some teachers simply do not care what their
students think of their teaching. If a system is introduced in which the
results of the Student Survey affect the amount of teachers' salaries, they
will no longer be able to ignore the students' voices.

3. _____ They are convenient
as there is no need to physically meet. You can participate from different
locations. This means that there is no need to spend money on transport to
get together. It also saves time in getting to the venue. On the other hand, it
is affected by the network environment. It is also difficult to have informal
discussions about things outside the agenda of the meeting. It is also
difficult to get a sense of working as a team. Therefore, online and face-to-
face meetings should be used depending on the situation.

Task 2-4

4人程度のグループで、Task 2-3 で各人が書いた topic sentence を比較検討しましょう。

Topic sentence の前に introductory sentences をもってくることがあります。
Introductory sentences は、非常に一般的 (general) な statement から始め、無理なく
topic sentence の内容につながるように書きます。

Example

Today, personal computers, or PCs, are a standard tool for a lot of people. The
two most common types of personal computers are Macs and PCs. Both are
quite widely used, but there are a number of differences between them.

分析してみると次のようになっています。

Today, personal computers are a standard tool for a lot of people.
<very general>
↓
The two most common types of personal computers are Macs and PCs.
<somewhat specific>
↓
Both are quite widely used, but there are a number of differences between them.
<topic sentence>

次の文が topic sentence である場合に、読者をそこまで導く introductory sentences を書
いてみましょう。

1. Young people today seem to have no reservations about meeting people on
   matching apps.

2. People should stop believing that being thin is a good thing.

3. Students should not be falling into debt because of scholarships.

4. If you only read news on social media, you will become a person with a
   biased point of view.

📘 Focusing on Form

Spacing

手書きの時はそれほど問題になりませんが、キーボードを使って英語を打つ際には、スペースの用い方に関する次のルールを守らねばなりません。

Rule 1　原則として punctuation marks（句読記号）は、直前の語のすぐ後に（スペースで隔てずに）置く。

    ×　What do you think of my opinion ?

    ○　What do you think of my opinion?

Rule 2　原則として punctuation marks の後には、スペースを１つ置く。

    ×　In my opinion,his argument was rather weak. The judge was not convinced.

    ○　In my opinion, his argument was rather weak. The judge was not convinced.

  ＊ **Rule 2** の例外　略号の内部に用いるピリオド（例えば、"U.S.A." の最初の２つのピリオド）の後にはスペースを置かない。アポストロフィの後にも置かない。

    ×　The session started at 9 a. m. and ended at 2 p. m.

    ○　The session started at 9 a.m. and ended at 2 p.m.

Rule 3　quotation marks (" "), brackets (( )) などの場合には、それらの囲みの中の要素との間にはスペースを置かない。囲みの外の要素との間にはスペースを１つ置く。

    ×　World Wildlife Fund(WWF)is addressing conservation issues.

    ○　World Wildlife Fund (WWF) is addressing conservation issues.

Rule 4　ハイフン (-)、ダッシュ (—) の前後にはスペースを置かない。（なお、ダッシュは２つの連続したハイフンとしてタイプすればよい。）

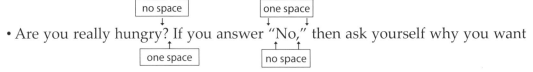

• Are you really hungry? If you answer "No," then ask yourself why you want

to eat when your body is not really hungry.

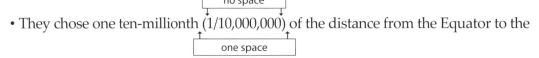

• They chose one ten-millionth (1/10,000,000) of the distance from the Equator to the

North Pole.

- Because there are no written records, we can't be certain. However,

  | one space | | one space | no space |

  there is one interesting fact.

Now *you* try!

次の文の spacing が適切になるように修正しましょう。本来スペースをとるべきところに
スペースがない場合には ∨、スペースをとるべきでないところにスペースがある場合には
∧ という記号を付してください。

1. Although people talk about the northern Kanto Region dialect , Ibaraki

   dialect , Tochigi dialect , and Gunma dialect are different from each other.

2. In my opinion , non-governmental organizations (NGOs) have a lot of

   important roles to play in today's international community. What do you

   think ?

3. The president said at the press conference , "We will not rule out any

   means in order to uproot terrorists . "

Writing Supporting Sentences
支持文で強力にサポート

この Unit では Supporting Sentences の書き方について、
さらに詳しく学習します。

Unit 1 では、supporting sentences については、おおよそ次のような説明がなされました。

The topic sentence should be supported by the rest of the sentences in the paragraph, which are called supporting sentences. Supporting sentences usually present several major points.

Task 3-1

🔊 Audio 09

音声もしくは先生の説明を聞き、良い supporting sentences の特徴をメモしましょう。

Task 3-2

A)〜C) のパラグラフには supporting sentences として不適当なものが含まれています。どの文が不適当なのかを見極め、なぜ不適当なのか説明しましょう。

A)   There are several reasons why running is the sport for me. Firstly, it is a sport that I can do alone. I don't need to find someone to do it with. I can do it whenever it suits me. Secondly, it is something I can do anywhere as long as there is a road there. Swimming is another sport that can be done alone, but you need to go to a swimming pool. I don't need to go to a special facility to run. Thirdly, it is a relatively inexpensive sport to do.

The only equipment you need is a pair of running shoes. To avoid getting injured, it's important to choose shoes that suit your level.

B)   Being a university student is challenging. First of all, it is academically demanding. The courses require much more reading and writing than in high school. It is a good opportunity to learn new things and broaden your horizons. Secondly, it is financially challenging. College tuition can be expensive and many students have to work part-time to pay for tuition, books and living expenses. Thirdly, it is psychologically challenging. College can be a big change and students may find it difficult to adjust to the new environment.

C)   Japanese junior and senior high schools have too many unreasonable rules. For example, most schools only allow black hair. Students with brownish hair have to prove that it's their natural color. Unbelievable! In addition, many schools forbid certain hairstyles, claiming that unique hairstyles will cause distraction and trouble. Nonsense! However, it is important to note that whether such a rule is considered unreasonable depends on the cultural background. The worst case is when schools only allow white underwear! What color underwear is worn is none of the schools' business.

Task 3-3

次の topic sentence に対する supporting sentences を、それぞれ３つ書いてみましょう。

1. You should be careful about several things when signing a contract.

    * _____

    * _____

    * _____

2. Some tools are indispensable in our lives.

    * _____

    * _____

-
_____

3. Several things have changed in me since I became a university student.
   -
_____
   -
_____
   -
_____

4. Different students have different reasons for joining clubs and circles.

   -
_____
   -
_____
   -
_____

5. It is important for us to go to elections for several reasons.

   -
_____
   -
_____
   -
_____

📖 Focusing on Form

Capitalization

大文字の使用に関して、これまでよく知っているものの他に、ここでは**タイトル**に使用するときのルールを覚えましょう。

Rule 1 すべての「主要な」語は大文字で始める。冠詞、前置詞、接続詞以外のすべての語は「主要な」語である。

Rule 2 品詞にかかわらず、4文字以上の語は「主要な」語と見なし、大文字で始める。

Rule 3 品詞にかかわらず、タイトルの最初の語は大文字で始める。

＊なお、タイトルは通常中央揃え（centering）にします。

Now *you* try!

パラグラフのタイトルとして適切になるよう、必要な文字を大文字にしましょう。

1. my favorite novelist

2. my scariest experience

3. why I think university tuition should be free

4. how best to choose a career

5. the problem of underage drinking

6. tips on choosing a course

Writing a Concluding Sentence
結論文で念押し

このUnitでは、効果的なConcluding Sentenceの書き方を
練習します。

Unit 1 では、concluding sentence については、おおよそ次のような説明がなされました。

The concluding sentence of a paragraph restates the main idea, using somewhat different words from the topic sentence.

Unit 1 での最初のモデルパラグラフ (p. 3) の topic sentence (TS) と concluding sentence (CS) は、それぞれ以下のようでした。

TS: Singing English songs is a good way to improve your English pronunciation.

CS: Therefore, if you want to make your pronunciation better, you should practice singing in English.

Task 4-1

🔊 Audio 10

先生の説明あるいは音声を聞いて、concluding sentence を書く際のコツについてメモしましょう。

Technique 1: _____

   Example _____

Technique 2: _____

   Example _____

Technique 3: _____

   Example _____

Concluding Phrases:

_____

_____

Task 4-2

1～9 の topic sentence に対応する concluding sentence を、それぞれ Technique 1 (T1) によって２つ、Technique 3 (T3) によって１つ、書いてみましょう。

1. Skiing is different from snowboarding in several ways.

   → T1: _____

   → T1: _____

   → T3: _____

2. Different age groups tend to use different social media platforms.

   → T1: _____

   → T1: _____

   → T3: _____

3. Tablet computers have several advantages over smartphones.

   → T1: _____

   → T1: _____

   → T3: _____

4. Professor X's course is very popular for many reasons.

   → T1: _____

   → T1: _____

   → T3: _____

5. A growing percentage of people in Japan remain single throughout their lives.

   → T1: _____

   → T1: _____

   → T3: _____

6. One of the key concepts that educational institutions need to promote is inclusiveness.

→ T1: _____

→ T1: _____

→ T3: _____

7. I would recommend this university to prospective students for three main reasons.

→ T1: _____

→ T1: _____

→ T3: _____

8. In my daily life, it is quite difficult to get seven hours of sleep.

→ T1: _____

→ T1: _____

→ T3: _____

9. People prefer to wear masks for a variety of reasons.

→ T1: _____

→ T1: _____

→ T3: _____

Task 4-3

次は、Task 4-2 の topic sentence に対応して学生が書いた concluding sentence ですが、誤りを含むものもあるようです。誤りがある場合には直してみましょう。

1. In these way, skiing differ from snowboarding.

2. In brief, people chooses social media platform according to their age.

3. Indeed, I recommend to take Professor X's course by all means.

Task 4-4

(1) 4人程度のグループで、Task 4-2で各人が書いた concluding sentence を比較検討しましょう。

(2) 1〜9のそれぞれについて、グループ内の、Technique 1, Technique 3による最優秀 concluding sentence を決めましょう。

(3) グループごとに最優秀 concluding sentence を発表し、クラス内の最優秀作を決めましょう。

📖 Focusing on Form

Fragments

それだけでは独立したセンテンスにならないのに、大文字で始めてピリオド等で終え、センテンスのような外観にしてしまっているものを、**fragments**（破片）と呼びます。fragments は誤りです。日本人学習者がつい書きがちである fragments の代表的なものに、次のようなもの（下線部）があります。

a. I don't think that speaking skills should be tested on the entrance exam for high school. <u>Because speaking is difficult to assess reliably.</u>

b. Recent political news has been disappointing. <u>For example, corruption, mistakes and favoritism.</u>

それぞれ次のように修正してセンテンスにする必要があります。

a'-1. I don't think that speaking skills should be tested on the entrance exam for high school **because** speaking is difficult to assess reliably.

a'-2. I don't think that speaking skills should be tested on the entrance exam for high school. **That is because** speaking is difficult to assess reliably.

b'-1. Recent political news has been disappointing. **For example, there have been** many reports of corruption, mistakes and favoritism.

b'-2. Recent political news — **corruption, mistakes and favoritism, for example** — has been disappointing.

Now *you* try !

1 〜 4 の文章中の fragments を見つけて、正しく直しましょう。

1. We have a Pepper. One of our precious family members.

   _____

2. I want to live the way I want to. Because only one life.

   _____

3. There are many things we need to be careful about when posting photos on social media. For example, other people's faces.

   _____

   _____

4. When I was in high school, I had to get up at 4 a.m. Because I had club activity in the morning every day.

   _____

   _____

   _____

The Process of Paragraph Writing

これまでは product（完成品）としてのパラグラフの構成を学習してきました。しかしパラグラフは一気に product として完成するわけではありません。普通、次のような process（過程）を経て作られるのです。

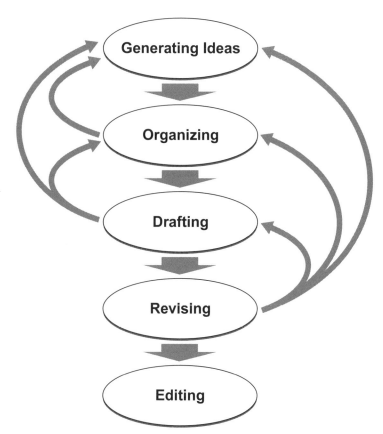

Generating Ideas

パラグラフを書くためには、まず書く材料がなければなりません。書くべき材料を考え出す（generate する）のがこの作業です。そのためには、あるトピックについて思いつくことをどんどんメモしてゆくのが効果的です。この段階では、順番、重要度の差、英語表現の正確さなどはあまり気にせず、思いつくままに出来る限りたくさんメモするのがコツです。この作業は Brain Storming とも呼ばれます。

Example 1 Clustering

Example 2 Listing

singing English songs
favorite songs
a range of music styles and genre
pop, rock, hip-hop, dance music
connect with listeners
great form of art
improve pronunciation
add/insert extra vowel
natural connected speech
full of linking, deletion, sound changes
iconic artists
the Beatles, Ed Sheeran, Lady Gaga, Bruno Mars
loved by people
meaningful lyrics
thought-provoking, touching
number of syllables = number of notes
same words and phrases
pronounce smoothly

TASK 1

次のトピック（あるいは自分の好きなトピック）からひとつ選び、思いつく idea を、英語（または日本語）で出来る限りたくさん、3分間で書いてみましょう。

- What Kind of People I Admire
- Behavior I Hate in People
- Why I Like This University
- What I Think Should Be Changed at This University

Organizing

思いつきをすべて並べたのでは、第三者に理解しやすいパラグラフは書けません。パラグラフに含める内容の構成を整えるのがOrganizing です。Generating Ideas でリストアップした ideas の中から、まず中心となる命題、main idea を決めます。その後で、ideas の中から、main idea をサポートするために使えるものだけを選びます。

今仮に main idea を Singing English songs is effective for improving pronunciation. だとすると、サポートとして使えそうなのは次のものです。

singing English songs
favorite songs
~~a range of music styles and genre~~
~~pop, rock, hip-hop, dance music~~
~~connect with listeners~~
~~great form of art~~
improve pronunciation
add/insert extra vowel
natural connected speech
full of linking, deletion, sound changes
~~iconic artists~~
~~the Beatles, Ed Sheeran, Lady Gaga, Bruno Mars~~
~~loved by people~~
~~meaningful lyrics~~
~~thought-provoking, touching~~
number of syllables = number of notes
same words and phrases
pronounce smoothly

残った ideas を使い、次のような形でパラグラフの骨組みを表わしたものを Outline と呼びます。

> Main Idea: Singing English songs is effective for improving pronunciation.
> 1. favorite songs; pronounce the same words many times; pronounce smoothly
> 2. can practice natural, connected speech, linking and deletion; sound changes
> 3. get syllables correct; number of syllables = number of notes

TASK 2

もし、main idea が、English songs are a great form of art. だとしたら、どうでしょうか。

(1) その場合に使える ideas を選んでみましょう。

(2) 残った ideas を、いくつかのポイントに構成して Outline の形にしてみましょう。

singing English songs
favorite songs
a range of music styles and genre
pop, rock, hip-hop, dance music
connect with listeners
great form of art
improve pronunciation
add/insert extra vowel
natural connected speech
full of linking, deletion, sound changes
iconic artists
the Beatles, Ed Sheeran, Lady Gaga, Bruno Mars
loved by people
meaningful lyrics
thought-provoking, touching
number of syllables = number of notes
same words and phrases
pronounce smoothly

このように、何を main idea にするかによって、パラグラフに含めるべき supporting ideas は変わってきます。逆に言えば、含めたい supporting ideas によって、main idea を変えなければならないのです。

TASK 3

Task 1 で自分がリストアップした ideas を眺め、
（1）main idea をひとつ決め、
（2）その main idea をサポートする ideas だけを選び、
（3）選んだ ideas を、Outline の形に構成してみましょう。

Drafting

Outline ができたら、それをとりあえず英語にしてみましょう。この段階では、英語表現に悩むよりは、全体の構成がしっかりしているかどうかに意識を集中することが大切です。（この点を強調するため、以下の Task で提示している sample drafts では、最終稿に至るまでは、**英語表現が不充分な点を敢えて残しています。**）

TASK 4

Task 3 で作った Outline にそって、Draft 1（第 1 稿）を書いてみましょう。

Draft 1 **Example**

Singing English songs is a good way to improve your English pronunciation. Singing your favorite songs will lead to pronouncing same words and phrases many times. You will learn to pronounce them smoothly. Singing songs provide many opportunities to practice natural, connected speech. Songs are full of linking, deletion, and other sound changes. Singing helps you to get your syllables correct. Japanese speakers of English tend to add extra vowel after consonants. You can't sing well if you do that. Singing English songs, you will learn not to insert unnecessary vowels.

Revising

Draft 1 ができたら、まず内容面、全体の構成に意識を向けて眺めてみましょう。上の例では、introductory sentences と、concluding sentences を補うことにします。(この2つは不可欠な要素ではありませんが、ここでは補うことにしてみます。)

Draft 2 **Example**

Do you ever sing English song? Did you know that those who sing English song on daily basis often have natural English pronunciation? There are at least three reasons why singing English songs is a good way to improve your English pronunciation. Singing your favorite songs will lead to pronouncing same words and phrases many times. You will learn to pronounce them more smoothly. Singing song provide many opportunities to practice natural, connected speech. Songs are full of linking, deletion, and other sound changes, which you can practice when singing. Singing helps you to get your syllables correct. Japanese speakers of English tend to add extra vowel after consonants. You can't sing well if you do that. Because the number of notes in the melody is same as the number of syllables in the lyrics. Singing English songs, you will learn not to insert unnecessary vowels. For these reasons, you can learn how to pronounce English better through singing in English. Next time you go to karaoke, why not try an English song?

TASK 5

Draft 1 (**Example**) と Draft 2 (**Example**) を見比べ、Draft 2 で加筆修正された部分に下線を引いて確認してみましょう。

TASK 6

Task 4 で書いた自分の Draft 1 を revise して Draft 2 にしてみましょう。(クラスメートと交換してお互いの draft を見るのも大変有効な方法です。)

Draft 2 をもう一度見て、内容的にさらに加筆、修正、削除が必要であれば書き直します。次の例では、つなぎ言葉を補い、またいくつかの個所で表現を修正しました。

Draft 3 **Example**

　Do you ever sing English song? Did you know that EFL learners who sing English song on daily basis often have natural English pronunciation? There are at least three reasons why singing English songs is a good way to improve your English pronunciation. First, singing your favorite songs will lead to pronouncing same words and phrases many times. With practice, you will learn to pronounce them more smoothly and naturally. Second, singing song provide many opportunities to practice natural, connected speech. Songs are full of linking, deletion, and other sound changes, which you can practice when singing. Third, most importantly, singing helps you to get your syllables correct. Japanese EFL learners tend to add extra vowel after consonants. You can't sing well if you do that. Because the number of notes in the melody is same as the number of syllables in the lyrics. Singing English songs, you will learn not to insert unnecessary vowels. For these reasons, you can learn how to pronounce English better through singing in English. Next time you go to karaoke, why not try an English song?

TASK 7

Draft 2 (**Example**) と Draft 3 (**Example**) を見比べて、Draft 3 で加筆修正された部分に下線を引いて確認しましょう。

Draft 3 をもう一度、今度は英語表現上の細かい問題がないかを中心に検討し、加筆・修正をします。この例では、冠詞が抜けている箇所や、単数・複数のミス、動詞形のミスが発見されたので直しました。

Final Draft **Example**　　　　　　　　　　　　　　　　　　　　　　🔊 Audio 11

Three Reasons Why Singing Helps Improve Your English Pronunciation

Do you ever sing English songs? Did you know that EFL learners who sing English songs on a daily basis often have natural English pronunciation? There are at least three reasons why singing English songs is a good way to improve your English pronunciation. First, singing your favorite songs will lead to pronouncing the same words and phrases many times. With practice, you will learn to pronounce them more smoothly and naturally. Second, singing songs provides many opportunities to practice natural, connected speech. Songs are full of linking, deletion, and other sound changes, which you can pracice when singing. Third, most importantly, singing helps you to get your syllables correct. Japanese speakers of English tend to add extra vowels after consonants. You can't sing well if you do that. That is because the number of notes in the melody is the same as the number of syllables in the lyrics. Singing English songs, you will learn not to insert unnecessary vowels. For these reasons, you can learn how to pronounce English better through singing in English. Next time you go to karaoke, why not try an English song?

TASK 8

Draft 3 (**Example**) と、Final Draft (**Example**) を見比べて、Final Draft で加筆修正された部分に下線を引いて確認しましょう。

TASK 9

自分の Draft 2 をもう一度点検し、表現上のミスをできる限りなくして、Final Draft を作ってみましょう。(クラスメート同士で draft を交換して editing をする peer editing も非常に有効な方法です。)

≫ まとめ

ライティングは、一度書いて終わるのではなく、時間の許す限り revising と editing を繰り返して draft の完成度を高めてゆく、繰り返しのプロセス (a cyclical process) です。またその際、まず内容面、構成面に注意を集中して大枠を固めてから、次に文法ミスや表現の改善などの表層に注意を移す、という順番が大切です。もちろん文法ミスに気づいたならその時点で直せばよいのですが、木を見て森を見ず、ということになってはいけません。

Rule 1	*Writing is a cyclical process.*
Rule 2	*Organization first; grammar and mechanics later.*

Stage 2

Writing in a Paragraph Format

You are going to learn . . . write paragraphs that

describe your favorite place	(Unit 5);
describe your passion	(Unit 6);
express your opinion	(Unit 7);
give advice and instructions	(Unit 8);
compare and contrast two things	(Unit 9);
explain Japanese things	(Unit 10);
narrate past events	(Unit 11); and
describe data expressed in graphs	(Unit 12).

UNIT

5

Describing Your Favorite Place

その街のどこが好きですか？

このUnitではある特定の場所・エリア（好きな街、よく利用する駅、大学の最寄り駅、故郷の町、架空の駅、など書きやすいものでよい）を説明するパラグラフを書きましょう。

まず説明する「場所」を決め、次のそれぞれの形容詞が、その「場所」に当てはまる度合いを選んでください。

extremely	very	rather	not very	not at all	
5	4	3	2	1	bustling
5	4	3	2	1	charming
5	4	3	2	1	commercial
5	4	3	2	1	contemporary
5	4	3	2	1	modern
5	4	3	2	1	clean
5	4	3	2	1	academic
5	4	3	2	1	cultural
5	4	3	2	1	convenient
5	4	3	2	1	crowded
5	4	3	2	1	lively
5	4	3	2	1	entertaining
5	4	3	2	1	energetic
5	4	3	2	1	fashionable
5	4	3	2	1	trendy
5	4	3	2	1	modern
5	4	3	2	1	vibrant
5	4	3	2	1	peaceful
5	4	3	2	1	quiet
5	4	3	2	1	historical
5	4	3	2	1	ancient
5	4	3	2	1	traditional
5	4	3	2	1	populous

5 —— 4 —— 3 —— 2 —— 1				dynamic
5 —— 4 —— 3 —— 2 —— 1				thriving
5 —— 4 —— 3 —— 2 —— 1				industrial
5 —— 4 —— 3 —— 2 —— 1				agricultural
5 —— 4 —— 3 —— 2 —— 1				residential
5 —— 4 —— 3 —— 2 —— 1				green
5 —— 4 —— 3 —— 2 —— 1				beautiful
5 —— 4 —— 3 —— 2 —— 1				hilly
5 —— 4 —— 3 —— 2 —— 1				mountainous
5 —— 4 —— 3 —— 2 —— 1				picturesque
5 —— 4 —— 3 —— 2 —— 1				quiet
5 —— 4 —— 3 —— 2 —— 1				deserted
5 —— 4 —— 3 —— 2 —— 1				safe
5 —— 4 —— 3 —— 2 —— 1				scenic
5 —— 4 —— 3 —— 2 —— 1				spacious

Task 5-2 ▶ Writing Concluding Sentences

Task 5-1 のスケールで、○をつけた位置が最も左であった語を３つ選び、次の _____ に書きましょう。

[場所の名前] is a place that can be described by three adjectives: _____, _____, and _____.

これが今回の topic sentence になります。

Task 5-3 ▶ Writing Introductory Sentences

Topic sentence に読者を導くための introductory sentences を書きましょう。topic sentence よりも general な内容で始め、topic sentence につながるよう工夫します。

· Different neighborhoods have different characteristics. <general>
· Understanding the characteristics of a neighborhood is important when choosing a place to live or visit. <specific>
· [   ] is place that can be characterized by three adjectives: _____,
   _____, and _____.

Task 5-4　▶ Outlining

Task 5-2 で選んだ３つの形容詞それぞれについて、その特徴の説明や実例となるようなことがらをそれぞれ、メモの形で書いてみましょう。

Example

1. convenient … close to the Yamanote Line / no worries after meals in the city center
2. stylish … spacious park / families and children relax / cosmopolitan restaurants
3. vibrant … young people / business people and students / eating and drinking late

Task 5-5　▶ Writing Supporting Sentences

Task 5-4 でたてたポイントのひとつひとつを、それぞれ２つのセンテンスで表現しましょう。最初のセンテンスは、比較的 general に、２番目のセンテンスは比較的 specific な内容にします。

Example

1. convenient … close to Shinjuku / no worries about getting home

   • It is convenient because it is rather close to the Yamanote Line <general>
   • I don't have to worry about getting home after a meal in the city center. <specific>

2. stylish … spacious park / families and children relax / cosmopolitan restaurants

   • It is stylish because there is a newly developed spacious park near the station. <general>
   • On weekends, families and children relax on the grass and dine at

cosmopolitan restaurants. <specific>
3. vibrant ⋯ young people / business people and students / eating and
        drinking late
    • The area is vibrant with energetic young people. <general>
    • Business people and university students enjoy eating and drinking late
      into the night. <specific>

Task 5-6 ▶ Talking in Pairs

Task 5-5 で書いた outline を利用して、ペアで話す練習をしてみましょう。

Example

A： How would you describe Nakano? What kind of place is it?

B： Well, first of all, it is convenient. It's rather close to the Yamanote Line. Only
   7 minutes from Shinjuku.

A： 7 minutes! That's close.

B： Yes, so if you live in Nakano, you don't have to worry about going back
   home after meeting someone in the city center.

A： That's true.

B： It's also a stylish place. There's a spacious park near the station. It's newly
   developed and there are cosmopolitan restaurants around it.

A： That's nice.

B： On weekends, families and children relax on the grass. And lastly, it is a
   vibrant town.

A： Vibrant? In what way?

B： There are lots of young people. They enjoy eating and drinking late into the
   night.

A： So, Nakano is convenient, stylish, and vibrant.

B： Yes. Now it's your turn. Which place are you going to tell me about?

A： Well, ...

40 —— Stage 2

Task 5-7 ▸ Writing Concluding Sentences

Unit 4 で学んだ３つのテクニークで、concluding sentence を書いてみましょう。

Example

Technique 1 (Restating the topic sentence):
Thus, these three adjectives will give you a good idea about what kind of town Nakano is.

Technique 2 (Summarizing the main points):
To summarize, Nakano is conveniently located, stylish, and vibrant.

Technique 3 (Giving a final thought):
For these reasons, Nakano is undoubtedly an attractive place to be both a resident and a visitor.

Task 5-8 ▸ Putting It All Together

🔊 Audio 13

いままで書いた文を改めてパラグラフにまとめましょう。構成を明確にするためのつなぎ言葉も使いましょう。

Example

Words That Best Describe Nakano

Different neighborhoods have different characteristics. Understanding the characteristics of a neighborhood is important when choosing a place to live or visit. One of the areas popular with young people is Nakano, where I live. Nakano is a place that can be characterized by three adjectives. Firstly, it is convenient because it is rather close to the Yamanote Line — just seven minutes from Shinjuku. I don't have to worry about getting home after a meal in the city center. Secondly, it is a stylish place as there is a newly developed spacious park with cosmopolitan restaurants near the station. On weekends, families and children relax on the grass and couples dine there. Finally, the area is vibrant with energetic young people crowding the unique shops and eateries. Businesspeople and university students enjoy eating and drinking late into the night near the station. For these reasons, Nakano is undoubtedly an attractive place to be both a resident and a visitor.

Words That Best Describe [   ]

_____

_____

[   ] is a place that can be characterized by three adjectives. First of all, it is a

_____ place because _____

_____ [   ] is also a(n) _____ place _____

_____.

Finally, the area is _____. To summarize, _____

_____.

自分の（あるいはパートナーの）パラグラフについて、以下の点をチェックしましょう。

Paragraph Level Check Points

- The first few sentences introduce the general background of the topic.

  ☐ Yes   ☐ Not sure ☐ No

- The paragraph has a topic sentence that tells the reader what the paragraph is about and what the writer wants to say about it.

  ☐ Yes   ☐ Not sure ☐ No

- The paragraph has good supporting sentences that elaborate on the main idea by giving further explanations, reasons, or examples.

  ☐ Yes   ☐ Not sure ☐ No
  There are (   ) supporting sentences.

- Transition words are used appropriately to make the organization clear.

  ☐ Yes   ☐ Not sure ☐ No

- The paragraph has a good concluding sentence that paraphrases the topic sentence, summarizes the main points, or gives a final comment on the topic.

  ☐ Yes   ☐ Not sure ☐ No

Sentence Level Check Points

Nouns
- Check if all the nouns are used appropriately, in their singular or plural forms, and with or without articles or other determiners.

  ☐ Done
  — found (   ) mistakes

Subject-Verb Agreement
- Check if the subjects and verbs agree in number.

  ☐ Done
  — found (   ) mistakes

Tense
- Check if the tenses of all the verbs are appropriate.

  ☐ Done
  — found (   ) mistakes

▐ Focusing on Form

Articles & Nouns

名詞は countable か uncountable かを常に意識することが必要です。また、冠詞その他の限定詞が必要か必要でないかも常に気にしましょう。

Now *you* try*!*

次のセンテンスは名詞がすべて単数形でかつ「裸」です。例にならい、必要に応じて語形を変えたり、語を補ったりしてください。

Ex) Some people treat baby stroller on bus and train as nuisance.

   → Some people treat baby **strollers** on buses and trains as **a** nuisance.

1. Taking long bath is good way to get rid of stress.

2. When you do different kind of sport, you can use different muscle.

3. I wonder if having student evaluate class at end of semester is meaningful.

4. It is unnerving to think that many animal are disappearing due to global warming.

5. When you write report, be sure to cite all your source.

6. On social media, you are only shown thing you want to read because of algorithm.

7. It is estimated that if world population keeps growing at current rate, it will reach 9.8 billion by year 2050.

8. People usually do not have pig or cow in mind when they eat pork or beef.

9. There must be a lot more child abuse than is reported in media.

Describing Your Passion
今、何に力を入れているの？

この Unit では今自分がハマっていること、情熱を燃やして
やっていることを紹介するパラグラフを書きましょう。

以下の事柄・活動についてあなたがどの程度「情熱を燃やして」いるか、○をつけましょう。

extremely   very   rather   not very   not at all

5 — 4 — 3 — 2 — 1	studies in my academic major
5 — 4 — 3 — 2 — 1	studies outside my academic major
5 — 4 — 3 — 2 — 1	studying for qualifying exams
5 — 4 — 3 — 2 — 1	learning languages
5 — 4 — 3 — 2 — 1	traveling
5 — 4 — 3 — 2 — 1	volunteering
5 — 4 — 3 — 2 — 1	sports club activities
5 — 4 — 3 — 2 — 1	fitness and health
5 — 4 — 3 — 2 — 1	reading fictions
5 — 4 — 3 — 2 — 1	writing fictions
5 — 4 — 3 — 2 — 1	composing music
5 — 4 — 3 — 2 — 1	playing musical instruments
5 — 4 — 3 — 2 — 1	music group(s)/band
5 — 4 — 3 — 2 — 1	singing/voice training
5 — 4 — 3 — 2 — 1	reading/writing poetry
5 — 4 — 3 — 2 — 1	painting/drawing
5 — 4 — 3 — 2 — 1	photography
5 — 4 — 3 — 2 — 1	dancing
5 — 4 — 3 — 2 — 1	cultural club activities
5 — 4 — 3 — 2 — 1	watching video-sharing websites
5 — 4 — 3 — 2 — 1	uploading to video-sharing sites
5 — 4 — 3 — 2 — 1	posting on Instagram
5 — 4 — 3 — 2 — 1	romantic love
5 — 4 — 3 — 2 — 1	working part-time
5 — 4 — 3 — 2 — 1	entrepreneurship/starting business
5 — 4 — 3 — 2 — 1	gender equality issues/activities
5 — 4 — 3 — 2 — 1	environmental issues/activities
5 — 4 — 3 — 2 — 1	social justice issues/activities
5 — 4 — 3 — 2 — 1	other political issues/activities

Task 6-2　　　Talking in Pairs

ペアになり、Task 6-1 で選んだ形容詞を使って、次のような形でやり取りをしてみましょう。

A： What is it that you are most passionate about now, other than your studies?

B： It's ＿＿＿＿＿＿＿＿.

A： Could you tell me about it?

B： Well, ＿＿＿＿＿＿＿＿＿＿＿＿＿＿＿＿＿＿＿＿＿＿＿＿＿＿＿

　　＿＿＿＿＿＿＿＿＿＿＿＿＿＿＿＿＿＿＿＿＿＿＿＿＿＿＿.

Example 1

🔊 Audio 14

A： What are you most passionate about at the moment, apart from your studies?

B： It's practicing breakdancing.

A： Could you tell me more about it?

B： Well, I belong to the dance club and now I am practicing breakdancing or breaking. Breaking has very acrobatic moves like spins, flips, and freezes. They are not easy, but when I have mastered a new move, it gives me a sense of accomplishment.

Example 2

A： What are you most passionate about at the moment, apart from your studies?

B： It's volunteering with a cat rescue group.

A： Could you tell me more about it?

B： Well, I'm a cat lover. A few years ago, I joined a group that tries to prevent the increase of stray cats. Our main activities are to catch stray cats, neuter them, and find people to adopt them. It's good for the cats as well as for the community.

Task 6-3　　　Writing a Topic Sentence

現在、一生懸命やっていることについて、次の形で表現しましょう。これが topic sentence のもとになります。

Example

My biggest passion outside of my studies at the moment is running.

My biggest passion outside of my studies at the moment is _____.

Task 6-4 ► Writing Introductory Sentences

Topic sentence に読者を導くための introductory sentences を書きましょう。topic sentence よりも general な内容で始め、topic sentence につながるよう工夫します。

Example

· Life is more fulfilling when you have something to be passionate about. <general>
· As a student, it is obviously important to be passionate about your studies, but it is better to have something else as well. <specific>
· My biggest passion outside of my studies at the moment is running.

Task 6-5 ► Outlining

自分が一所懸命やっている活動についてメモをアウトラインの形にまとめましょう。

Example

· running
· why I started – too much fat on my belly – sit-ups NG – aerobic activities
· concerns
  (1) weak knees
     → supporting tights
  (2) monotonous
     → running watch w/ GPS – recorded where, how fast, how far – great encouragement
       ability improved – 200K/month

Task 6-6 ► Writing Supporting Sentences

Task 6-5 で書いたメモをみながら、Task 6-3 で書いた topic sentence をサポートする内容を文の形にしてみましょう。

Example

· I started running because I had too much fat on my belly.
· When I started, I had two concerns.

1. I had always had weak knees.
2. Isn't running monotonous? Can I continue?

· I found a pair of good supporting tights. I felt no pain at all.

· I bought a running watch with GPS. It recorded where, how fast, and how far I ran.

· It was a great encouragement. It prevented feeling bored while running.

· My running ability improved and now I run about 200 kilometers a month.

Task 6-7 ▶ Writing Concluding Sentences

Unit 4 で学んだ３つのテクニークで、concluding sentence を書いてみましょう。

Example

Technique 1 (Paraphrasing the topic sentence):

In this way, running has become my greatest passion apart from studying.

Technique 2 (Summarizing the main points):

Thus, I have managed to keep running supported by good running tights and motivated by a running watch.

Technique 3 (Giving a final thought):

Actually, I am thinking of running a full marathon next year!

いままで書いた文を改めてパラグラフにまとめましょう。文と文の関係を明確にするためのつなぎ言葉も使いましょう。

Example

What I Am Currently Into

Life is more fulfilling when you have something to be passionate about. As a student, it is obviously important to be passionate about your studies, but it is better to have something else as well. **My biggest passion outside of the classroom is long distance-running, which I started two years ago, for three reasons.** Firstly, running makes my body look better. Two years ago I was at my heaviest weight and my clothes were tight. But since I started running, I have gradually lost weight and now have a BMI of 22. My self-image has been restored and my self-esteem has increased. Secondly, **it actually improves my physical performance.** Unlike sprinting, with long-distance running, the more you run, the better you get. At first I couldn't even run two kilometers, but gradually my running distance and speed increased and now I can run 20 kilometers with no difficulty. As your ability to run improves, you want to improve even more. And finally, **running lets me spend every day with a purpose.** Races of various sizes are held somewhere every month and they are easy to enter as they are individual events. I spend my days practicing for the race I have entered, with the aim of beating my personal best. **In this way, long-distance running keeps me fit, improves my physical strength and gives me a sense of fulfilment every day**, which is why I am now an enthusiastic runner.

自分の（あるいはパートナーの）パラグラフについて、以下の点をチェックしましょう。

Paragraph Level Check Points

- The first few sentences introduce the general background of the topic.

  ☐ Yes ☐ Not sure ☐ No

- The paragraph has a topic sentence that tells the reader what the paragraph is about and what the writer wants to say about it.

  ☐ Yes ☐ Not sure ☐ No

- The paragraph has good supporting sentences that elaborate on the main idea by giving further explanations, reasons, or examples.

  ☐ Yes ☐ Not sure ☐ No
  There are ( ) supporting sentences.

- Transition words are used appropriately to make the organization clear.

  ☐ Yes ☐ Not sure ☐ No

- The paragraph has a good concluding sentence that paraphrases the topic sentence, summarizes the main points, or gives a final comment on the topic.

  ☐ Yes ☐ Not sure ☐ No

Sentence Level Check Points

Nouns
- Check if all the nouns are used appropriately, in their singular or plural forms, and with or without articles or other determiners.

  ☐ Done
  — found ( ) mistakes

Subject-Verb Agreement
- Check if the subjects and verbs agree in number.

  ☐ Done
  — found ( ) mistakes

Tense
- Check if the tenses of all the verbs are appropriate.

  ☐ Done
  — found ( ) mistakes

📖 Focusing on Form

Subject-Verb Agreement / Singular vs. Plural

言うまでもなく、主語と動詞の数は一致している必要があります。知識としては知っていても、実際に使えなければ意味がありません。

Now *you* try❗

1～10のセンテンスで使われている主語と動詞の対応はよいか、名詞は適当かを確認し、問題があれば直しましょう。ほかのタイプの誤りがある場合はそれも直しましょう。

1. Russia is one of the country that has nuclear weapon.

2. It has been about two and a half year since I entered into this college.

3. I don't think everyone in class agree on this issue.

4. There is several reason why Major League Baseball are popular in Japan.

5. Most people says that watching movie in movie theaters are the best way to enjoy, but is it a really true?

6. Not only watching games on internet but there is many way to make you exciting about sports.

7. The men in that black car was not dead but just slept.

8. Whoever say that I should quit, I will not. Because I don't want to be loser.

9. I am a 18-years-old woman who are planning to study in Australia.

10. Playing game is now one of the most interested hobby to me.

UNIT

7

Expressing an Opinion
学校に部活動なんていらない？!

このUnitでは、自分の意見を述べるパラグラフを
書いてみましょう。

次のチャートを見て、自分の意見に比較的近いことを述べているセンテンスを５つ選んでください。選んだら、そう思う理由をひとつずつ考えてください。

～するのは素晴らしい／悪くない／良いことではない

It is	an excellent idea a good idea not such a bad idea not a good idea a stupid idea	to	wear a mask all the time for non-health reasons. use dating apps to find a partner. put up too many "don't" signs in parks. make tuition fees to university completely free. regulate the use of AI in schools.

いまや～するべき時期だ／～するのはまだ適切でない

It is	high time not yet appropriate	for club activities to be transferred from schools to the community. for married couples to be allowed to have different surnames. for same-sex marriage to be legalized. for Japan to phase out coal-fired power generation. for a gender quota system for elections to be introduced.

許可されるべきだ／規制されるべきだ／禁止されるべきだ

Buying and selling animals as pets Walking up escalators Drinking in public places Doctor-assisted suicide Consuming whale meat Making hate speech	should be should not be	legalized. allowed. regulated. regulated more strictly. prohibited. banned as it is.

増やすべきだ／減らすべきだ

There should be	an increase a decrease	in the number of	university courses available online. refugees admitted into Japan. students in English classes. gender-neutral toilets. smoke-free buildings and facilities.

Task 7-2 ▷ Talking in Pairs　　　　　　　　　　🔊 Audio 16

Task 7-1 で選んだセンテンスを利用して、ペアで話す練習をしてみましょう。

Example 1

A : It is not a good idea to wear a mask all the time for non-health reasons.

B : Why do you think so?

A : Because it makes it harder for other people to communicate with that person.

B : Really? I don't think so.

Example 2

A : It is high time for club activities to be transferred from schools to the community.

B : Why do you think so?

A : Because it's not the job of the teachers to be in charge of extra-curricular activities in the first place.

B : Then whose jobs should it be?

Task 7-3 ▷ Writing a Topic Sentence

Task 7-2 で練習したセンテンスの中からひとつ選び、In my opinion, ... / I strongly believe that ... に続けて書きましょう。これが topic sentence となります。

Example

In my opinion, it is high time for club activities to be transferred from schools to the community.

Task 7-4 ▷ Writing Introductory Sentences

Topic sentence に読者を導くための introductory sentences を書きましょう。topic sentence よりも general な内容で始め、topic sentence につながるよう工夫します。

Example

・Today, there is a general perception that teachers suffer from a poor work/life balance. <general>

・The main reason for this is that they have to spend an excessive amount of time on after-school club activities. <specific>

Task 7-5 ▶ Outlining

Task 7-3 で書いた topic sentence の内容を読者に納得させるためのポイントを2つ以上考え、次のようなメモの形で書きましょう。この段階では英語表現に悩むより、内容的に説得力のある理由を立てることに集中してください。

Example

1. legally … subject … teaching license … no such thing … license to run a volleyball club
2. virtually unpaid … after 5pm … weekends … no one … forced to work … against their will
3. alienates … candidates … love to teach … club activities before teaching

Task 7-6 ▶ Talking in Pairs   📶 Audio 17

Task 7-5 で書いた outline を利用して、ペアで話す練習をしてみましょう。

Example

A : I think club activities should be moved out of schools and into the community.

B : Oh. Why do you think that?

A : The first reason is license. Teachers can teach subjects in schools because they have licenses to teach those subjects. But there is no such thing as a license to run club activities. This means that no teacher has the expertise to run clubs.

B : Okay. I see.

A : The second thing is the working conditions. Teachers have to work long hours during the week and even on weekends. Many of them have only one or two days off a month! That's because they have to take care of club activities on Saturdays and Sundays! And they are practically unpaid for those overtime hours!

B : That's terrible.

<The interaction continues>

Task 7-7 ▷ Writing Supporting Sentences

Task 7-5 でたてたポイントのひとつひとつを、それぞれ２つのセンテンスで表現してください。最初のセンテンスは、比較的 general に、２番目のセンテンスは比較的 specific な内容にします。

Example

1. legally ... subject ... teaching license ... no such thing ... license to run a volleyball club
   - Teachers are legally allowed to teach only the subject for which they have a teaching license.
   - There is no such thing as a license to run a volleyball club, for example.

2. virtually unpaid ... after 5pm ... weekends ... no one ... forced to work ... against will
   - Teachers are virtually unpaid for the work they do after 5pm on weekdays and on weekends.
   - No one should be forced to work unpaid against their will.

3. alienates ... candidates ... love to teach ... club activities before teaching
   - The current situation alienates teacher candidates who would love to teach subjects.
   - Only those who put club activities before teaching will become teachers.

Task 7-8 ▷ Writing Concluding Sentences

Unit 4 で学んだ３つのテクニークで concluding sentence を書いてみましょう。

Example

Technique 1 (Paraphrasing the topic sentence):
   In conclusion, schools should stop being responsible for running club activities and hand that responsibility over to the outside community.

Technique 2 (Summarizing the main points):
   To sum up, teachers should not be forced to work long hours, unpaid, which discourages potentially capable teachers from becoming teachers.

Technique 3 (Giving a final thought):
   If schools do not attract those who would be good at teaching, the academic abilities of students will suffer.

いままで書いた文を改めてパラグラフにまとめましょう。構成を明確にするためのつなぎ言葉も使いましょう。

School Teachers Should Say Goodbye to Clubs

Today, there is a general perception that teachers suffer from a poor work/life balance. The main reason for this is that they have to spend an excessive amount of time on after-school club activities. In my opinion, it is high time to shift club activities from schools to the community. **Firstly**, teachers are legally allowed to teach only the subject for which they have a teaching license. There is no such thing as a licence to run a volleyball club, for example. Forcing teachers to do work that has nothing to do with their license is an insult to their professionalism. **Secondly**, teachers are virtually unpaid for the work they do after 5pm on weekdays and on weekends. No one should be forced to work unpaid against their will. Such an inhumane schedule naturally takes a toll on teachers' family lives and their mental and physical well-being. **Thirdly**, and most importantly, the current situation alienates teacher candidates who would love to teach subjects but abhor being in charge of a club. Only those who put club activities before teaching — putting the cart before the horse — will become teachers who need to get their priorities straight. **In conclusion**, schools should stop being responsible for running club activities as soon as possible and hand that responsibility over to the outside community. Otherwise, schools will not attract those who would be good at teaching, and the academic abilities of students will suffer.

自分の（あるいはパートナーの）パラグラフについて、以下の点をチェックしましょう。

Paragraph Level Check Points

- The first few sentences introduce the general background of the topic.

  ☐ Yes ☐ Not sure ☐ No

- The paragraph has a topic sentence that tells the reader what the paragraph is about and what the writer wants to say about it.

  ☐ Yes ☐ Not sure ☐ No

- The paragraph has good supporting sentences that elaborate on the main idea by giving further explanations, reasons, or examples.

  ☐ Yes ☐ Not sure ☐ No
  There are ( ) supporting sentences.

- Transition words are used appropriately to make the organization clear.

  ☐ Yes ☐ Not sure ☐ No

- The paragraph has a good concluding sentence that paraphrases the topic sentence, summarizes the main points, or gives a final comment on the topic.

  ☐ Yes ☐ Not sure ☐ No

Sentence Level Check Points

Nouns
- Check if all the nouns are used appropriately, in their singular or plural forms, and with or without articles or other determiners.

  ☐ Done
  — found ( ) mistakes

Subject-Verb Agreement
- Check if the subjects and verbs agree in number.

  ☐ Done
  — found ( ) mistakes

Tense
- Check if the tenses of all the verbs are appropriate.

  ☐ Done
  — found ( ) mistakes

📖 Focusing on Form

Tenses

時制の種類は知っていても、どの時制をどこで使うべきか、を誤解している人が多いようです。特に過去形を使うべき時に過去完了や現在完了を使ってしまうミスや、あるいはその逆のミスなどが多く見られます。

Now *you* try !

次の1～6は大学生が過去を振り返って書いたものです。時制の誤りがあれば直しましょう。他のタイプの誤りもあれば同時に直しましょう。

1. In my childhood, when I go to bed, Father always sing a song.

2. When I was high school students, I was belonging wind orchestra club.

3. When I was second grade in high school, I had been to U.K. for two months.

4. When I was high school, I remembered playing baseball with my friends.

5. I started school when I was four years old. I have been a student for sixteen years. I had studied Japanese, math, science, and so on in junior and senior high schools. I attend this university for one and a half year. I have been studied data science.

6. I had belonged to a swimming club when I was a high school student. I wanted to enter it in university. Therefore, since there is not it in this campus, I couldn't enter it. However, since I couldn't gave up entering it, now I am going to a swimming school near my apartment.

Giving Advice and Instructions

悪徳商法に引っかからないために

Pyramid Scher

このUnitでは、「××の効果的な方法」「○○のやり方」など、
物事の方法や手順について読み手にアドバイスするパラグラフ
を書きましょう。

Task 8-1 ► Generating Ideas

まず何の方法について書くかを考えましょう。自分がよく知っていることがよいでしょう。決まらない場合は、次の中から選ぶこともできます。

- How to write an effective job application
- How to live on 1,000 yen a day to eat
- How to live a fulfilling college life
- How to take quality photos with your smartphone
- How to make yourself look better in video meetings
- How to avoid falling victim to dishonest business practices

Task 8-2 ► Writing a Topic Sentence

上で選んだトピックについて、次のような文を書きましょう。これが topic sentence のもとになります。

パタン A: _____ ing will be easy if you follow these steps.

パタン B: To _____ , you should _____ .

パタン C: If you want to _____ , there are several things to remember.

Example

To avoid falling victim to dishonest business practices, you should beware of several situations.

Task 8-3 ► Writing Introductory Sentences

Topic sentence に読者を導くための introductory sentences を書きましょう。topic sentence よりも general な内容で始め、topic sentence につながるよう工夫します。

Example

· If you are 18 years old or older, you are an adult. <general>
· Unlike a minor, an adult can enter into various contracts without parental consent. <more specific>
· This may sound convenient, but it is also convenient for someone who wants to extort money from you. <more specific>

· To avoid falling victim to dishonest business practices, you should beware of several situations.

<Peer Advising>
ペアでお互いの Introductory sentences を検討し、流れが general → specific となっているかを確認し、必要に応じてサジェスチョンを行ないましょう。

Task 8-4 ▶ Outlining

Topic sentence をサポートするポイントを箇条書きにした outline を書きましょう。

Example

1. approaches you / street / doing a survey
   somewhere else → fake
2. beware / too good to be true / dating app / spend money
   membership / travel / low cost → dating scam
3. pyramid scheme / lots of money / recruit others
   pay 10,000 yen to join a club / paid 20,000 yen / each new member

Task 8-5 ▶ Talking in Pairs 🔊 Audio 19

Task 8-4 で書いた outline を利用して、ペアのパートナーに向かって話す練習をしてみましょう。

Example

A: Imagine a man approaches you on the street. He says he's doing a quick survey of young people's shopping habits.

B: That happens.

A: But if, after the survey, he asks you to go somewhere else like a cafe, don't do it.

B: Why not?

A: It may be a "catch" sale. You may be trapped and end up buying an expensive product.

B: I see.

(*The interaction continues.*)

Task 8-4 でたてたポイントのひとつひとつを、それぞれ２つ以上のセンテンスで表現してください。最初のセンテンスは、instruction（指示）に、２番目以降のセンテンスは reason にします。

1. approaches you / street / do a survey
   somewhere else → catch sale
   • Beware if someone approaches you on the street, saying that they are doing a survey about something. <instruction>
   • After that, you may be invited to go somewhere else and be trapped in a "catch" sale of expensive products or services. <reason>

2. be alert / too good to be true / dating app / sign a contract
   membership / travel / low cost/ → dating scam
   • Be alert if someone too good to be true who you met through a dating app asks you to sign a contract. <instruction>
   • For example, he/she may ask you to buy a membership that allows you to travel together at a low cost, which could be a dating scam. <reason>

3. lots of money / recruit others
   pay 10,000 yen to join a club / paid 20,000 yen / each new member →
   pyramid scheme
   • Watch out if someone says that you can make lots of money by recruiting others. <instruction>
   • For example, you pay 10,000 yen to join a certain club, and you are paid 20,000 yen for each new member you recruit. That is called a "pyramid" scheme. <reason>

Task 8-7 ▶ Writing Concluding Sentences

Unit 4 で学んだ３つのテクニックで concluding sentence を書いてみましょう。

Example

Technique 1 (Restating the topic sentence):
   Thus, to avoid falling into the trap of unscrupulous business practices, you should be very watchful of these situations.

Technique 2 (Summarizing the main points):

To summarize, beware of street surveys, your dream boyfriend/girlfriend urging you to sign a contract, and easy money schemes.

Technique 3 (Giving a final thought):

The bottom line is to step back and think about it. If something is not right, have the courage to say no.

Task 8-8 ▶ Putting It All Together

📶 Audio 20

いままで書いた文を改めてパラグラフにまとめましょう。構成を明確にするためのつなぎ言葉も使いましょう。

Protect Yourself from Dishonest Businesses

If you are 18 years old or older, you are an adult. Unlike a minor, an adult can enter into various contracts without parental consent. This may sound convenient, but it is also convenient for someone who wants to extort money from you. **To avoid falling victim to dishonest business practices, you should beware of several situations**. First, beware if someone approaches you on the street, saying that they are doing a survey about something. After that, you may be invited to go somewhere else and be trapped in a "catch" sale of expensive products or services. **Secondly**, be alert if someone too good to be true who you met through a dating app asks you to sign a contract that benefits both of you. For example, he/she may ask you to buy a membership that allows you to travel together at a low cost. That could be a dating scam. **Thirdly**, watch out if someone says that you can make lots of money by recruiting others. For example, you pay 10,000 yen to join a certain club, and you are paid 20,000 yen for each new member you recruit. That is called a "pyramid" scheme. **To summarize, beware of street surveys, your dream boyfriend/girlfriend urging you to sign a contract, and easy money schemes**. There are numerous other cases too, but the bottom line is to step back and think about it. If something is not right, have the courage to say no.

自分の（あるいはパートナーの）パラグラフについて、以下の点をチェックしましょう。

Paragraph Level Check Points

- The first few sentences introduce the general background of the topic.

  ☐ Yes ☐ Not sure ☐ No

- The paragraph has a topic sentence that tells the reader what the paragraph is about and what the writer wants to say about it.

  ☐ Yes ☐ Not sure ☐ No

- The paragraph has good supporting sentences that elaborate on the main idea by giving further explanations, reasons, or examples.

  ☐ Yes ☐ Not sure ☐ No
  There are (   ) supporting sentences.

- Transition words are used appropriately to make the organization clear.

  ☐ Yes ☐ Not sure ☐ No

- The paragraph has a good concluding sentence that paraphrases the topic sentence, summarizes the main points, or gives a final comment on the topic.

  ☐ Yes ☐ Not sure ☐ No

Sentence Level Check Points

Nouns
- Check if all the nouns are used appropriately, in their singular or plural forms, and with or without articles or other determiners.

  ☐ Done
  — found (   ) mistakes

Subject-Verb Agreement
- Check if the subjects and verbs agree in number.

  ☐ Done
  — found (   ) mistakes

Tense
- Check if the tenses of all the verbs are appropriate.

  ☐ Done
  — found (   ) mistakes

📖 Focusing on Form

Run-Ons

２つ以上のセンテンスを単にコンマでつないで１つのセンテンスのようにしたもの (Run-ons) は誤りです。適切な接続詞でつなぐ必要があります。

× A famous branded bag is sold very cheaply, that is likely to be a fake.

○ If a famous branded bag is sold very cheaply, that is likely to be a fake.

○ When a famous branded bag is sold very cheaply, that is likely to be a fake.

次のような形も可能です。

○ A famous branded bag sold very cheaply is likely to be a fake.

Now *you* try !

次の１〜４の中に、Run-Ons があれば適切に直しましょう。

1. TikTok videos are funny, I waste hours just watching them.

　　_____

2. At high school, teachers tell you what to do and what not to do, at college, you can do anything you like.

　　_____

3. I work part-time, I do not have to be totally dependent on my parents.

　　_____

4. The current rate of fertility does not change, world population will reach 9.7 billion by the year 2050.

　　_____

Comparing and Contrasting
実家からの通学と一人暮らし

この Unit では、似ているけれど違う二つのものを比較対照するパラグラフを書いてみましょう。

Task 9-1 ▶ Generating Ideas

まず何と何を比較するかを考えましょう。あまり一般に指摘されていない違いがあるものがよいですね。決まらない場合は、次の中から選ぶこともできます。

- High School Teachers and University Teachers
- On-Demand Classes and Simultaneous Online Classes
- Skiing and Snowboarding
- NPB (Nippon Professional Baseball) and MLB (Major League Baseball)
- Smartphones and Laptops
- Online Meetings and Face-to-Face Meetings
- Living with Your Family and Living on Your Own

Task 9-2 ▶ Writing a Topic Sentence

上で選んだトピックについて、次のような文を書きましょう。これが topic sentence のもとになります。

パタン A: _____ and _____ are different [similar] in several (interesting / amusing / important) ways.

パタン B: _____ is different from [similar to] _____ in a number of (interesting / amusing / important) ways.

Example

Living alone is different from living with your family in several important ways.

Task 9-3 ▶ Writing Introductory Sentences

Topic sentence に読者を導くための introductory sentences を書きましょう。topic sentence よりも general な内容や、個人的なエピソードで始め、topic sentence につながるよう工夫します。

Example

・Last year I was coming to the university from my home in T Prefecture. <personal episode>
・This April I rented an apartment near the university, so I have been living on

my own for three months now. <personal episode>

· Living alone is different from living with your family in several important ways.

<Peer Advising>

ペアでお互いの Introductory sentences を検討し、うまく reader を topic sentence に導けているかを確認し、必要に応じてサジェスチョンを行ないましょう。

Task 9-4 ▶ Outlining

Topic sentence をサポートするポイントを箇条書きにした outline を書きましょう。

Example

1. time to come to uni
   before: 2.5 hrs × 2 / buses and trains / little time with friends
   now: 10 min / dancing / hanging out with friends
2. costs more
   before: only money = transportation / 30,000 yen / commuter pass / convenient
   now: rent / food / utilities = 100,000+ / more part-time
3. more freedom
   before: cannot invite anyone anytime casually
   now: the boss / more freedom → mess up routine / unhealthy life

Task 9-5 ▶ Talking in Pairs

Audio 21

Task 9-4 で書いた outline を利用して、ペアで話す練習をしてみましょう。

Example

A : I lived in T Prefecture with my family last year.

B : T Prefecture? How long did it take you to get here?

A : About two and a half hours.

B : Wow! So you spent about five hours on buses and trains?

A : Yes. I had to go home immediately after class, so I had little time to spend with my friends.

B : That's kind of sad.

A : But in April this year I left home and moved into an apartment just ten minutes away from the university.

(*The interaction continues.*)

Task 9-4 でたてたポイントのひとつひとつを、それぞれ２つ以上のセンテンスで表現してください。比較しているそれぞれの特徴に一つずつ触れるようにします。

Example

1. less time to get to uni

   before: 2.5 hrs × 2 / buses and trains / little time with friends

   now: 10 min / dancing / hanging out with friends

· It takes much less time to come to the university.

· When living in T Prefecture, it took about 2 and a half hours, each way. I could spend little time with my friends after class.

· Now it is only a ten-minute's walk from the university. I am enjoying practicing dancing in a circle and hanging out with my friends from time to time.

2. costs more

   before: only money = transportation / 30,000 yen

   now: rent / food / utilities = 100,000+

· Last year, the only money I had to pay was for transportation, which was about 30,000 yen.

· Now, the apartment rent, food expenses and utilities combined add up to more than 100,000 yen.

3. freer / better or worse

   before: couldn't just invite people

   now: you are the boss / more freedom → negative effect / unhealthy lifestyle

· You are freer, for better or for worse, when you live alone.

· When you live with your family, you can't just invite people into your room whenever you feel like it.

· When you live alone, you are the boss of your own household. But more freedom can also have a negative effect, making it easier to lead an unhealthy lifestyle.

Task 9-7 ► Writing Concluding Sentences

Unit 4 で学んだ３つのテクニークで、concluding sentence を書いてみましょう。

Example

Technique 1 (Restating the topic sentence):

Thus there are important differences between living with your family and living on your own.

Technique 2 (Summarizing the main points):

To summarize, living on your own gives you more time, costs you more money and allows you to enjoy more freedom—for better or for worse.

Technique 3 (Giving a final thought):

I am determined to use the extra time and freedom to develop into a more mature person.

Task 9-8 ► Putting It All Together

Audio 22

いままで書いた文を改めてパラグラフにまとめましょう。構成を明確にするためのつなぎ言葉も使いましょう。また、文のパタンが単調にならないよう、センテンスの始まりに変化をつけましょう。

Example

Differences Between Living Alone and Living with Your Parents

Last year I was coming to the university from my home in T Prefecture but this April I rented an apartment near the university. Having lived on my own for three months now, **I have found that living on my own is very different from living with my family in a number of important ways.** First of all, **it obviously takes much less time to get to the university.** When I lived in T Prefecture, it took about two and a half hours each way. Spending five hours a day on buses and trains was bad enough, but what was worse was having so little time with my friends after class. Now that I live a ten-minute's walk away from the university, I am a member of the dance club and enjoy hanging out with my friends from time to time. **Secondly, it costs more to live alone.** When I lived with my family, the only money I had to pay was for transportation, which was about 30,000 yen a month. Living alone, the apartment rent, food expenses and utilities combined add up to more than 100,000 yen. **Finally, you**

are obviously freer, for better or worse, when you live alone. When you live with your family, you can't just invite people into your room whenever you feel like it, but when you live alone, you are the boss of your own household. But more freedom can also have a negative effect, making it easier to lead an unhealthy lifestyle. To sum up, living alone gives you more time and freedom but costs you more money. As for me, I am determined to use the extra time and freedom to develop into a more mature person.

Task 9-9 ► Self/Peer Revising/Editing

自分の（あるいはパートナーの）パラグラフについて、以下の点をチェックしましょう。

Paragraph Level Check Points

- The first few sentences introduce the general background of the topic.

  ☐ Yes ☐ Not sure ☐ No

- The paragraph has a topic sentence that tells the reader what the paragraph is about and what the writer wants to say about it.

  ☐ Yes ☐ Not sure ☐ No

- The paragraph has good supporting sentences that elaborate on the main idea by giving further explanations, reasons, or examples.

  ☐ Yes ☐ Not sure ☐ No
  There are (   ) supporting sentences.

- Transition words are used appropriately to make the organization clear.

  ☐ Yes ☐ Not sure ☐ No

- The paragraph has a good concluding sentence that paraphrases the topic sentence, summarizes the main points, or gives a final comment on the topic.

  ☐ Yes ☐ Not sure ☐ No

Sentence Level Check Points

Nouns
- Check if all the nouns are used appropriately, in their singular or plural forms, and with or without articles or other determiners.

  ☐ Done
  — found (   ) mistakes

Subject-Verb Agreement
- Check if the subjects and verbs agree in number.

  ☐ Done
  — found (   ) mistakes

Tense
- Check if the tenses of all the verbs are appropriate.

  ☐ Done
  — found (   ) mistakes

📖 Focusing on Form

Choppiness (I)

あまりに短いセンテンスばかりを羅列すると、幼稚な印象を与えます。適切な従属接続詞や分詞構文等を使って、複文を作る努力が必要です。（注意：and, but, so などの等位接続詞だけで文をつないでも幼稚な印象は変わりません。）

Now *you* try !

例にならって、次の１〜５のそれぞれに含まれるすべての情報を、１センテンスで表してみましょう。

Example:　I forgot to put suntan lotion on my back. I got severely burned. I look like a piece of bacon.
→ Since I forgot to put suntan lotion on my back, I got severely burned and now look like a piece of bacon.

1. I am a Japanese woman. I am 20 years old. I am thinking of studying at a college in the U.K.

_____

_____

2. *Yakimanju* is a local specialty of Takasaki. Takasaki is my hometown. It is in Gunma. *Yakimanju* are steamed buns grilled with sweet and salty sauce.

_____

_____

3. My hometown is Katsunuma. It is in Yamanashi. It is located about 120 km northwest of Tokyo. It is a beautiful city. It is famous for wine production.

_____

_____

4. My aunt is an interesting person. Her name is Aoi Tanaka. She was born in China. She grew up in Russia. Now she lives in Tokyo. She is a co-founder of an NGO.

_____

_____

5. Dinosaurs dominated the earth for 140 million years. It was a long time. After that, they became extinct. What caused them to become extinct? What do you think?

_____

_____

UNIT

10

Explaining Japanese Culture
説明しよう、日本の文化

この Unit では、日本の文化や風習について
説明する練習をしましょう。

Task 10-1 ► Generating Ideas

まず日本文化の何について書くかを考えましょう。自分がよく知っていることがよいでしょう。決まらない場合は、次の中から選ぶこともできます。

- Temples and shrines
- Scenic beauty of the mountains
- Religious practices and ceremonies
- Japanese *onsen* - hot springs
- *Sumo* wrestling
- Traditional Japanese theatre — *Kabuki, Noh*
- Japanese pop culture (*manga, anime, otaku*)
- Tea ceremony
- Traditional Japanese delicacies
- Cheap but delicious local food
- Traditional Japanese clothing

Task 10-2 ► Writing a Topic Sentence

上で選んだトピックについて、次のような文を書きましょう。これが topic sentence のもとになります。

パタン A: _____ attract(s) many foreigners to Japan for good reason.

パタン B: _____ has/have some unique aspects that distinguish them from their counterparts in other countries.

パタン B: Tourists to Japan should not fail to try/watch/experience _____.

Example

Japanese *onsen* have several unique aspects that distinguish them from their counterparts in other countries.

Task 10-3 ► Writing Introductory Sentences

Topic sentence に読者を導くための introductory sentences を書きましょう。topic sentence よりも general な内容で始め、topic sentence につながるよう工夫します。

· In recent years, the number of foreign tourists visiting Japan has increased. <general>

· One of the most popular aspects of Japanese culture among foreigners is *onsen* (hot springs). <specific>

· Japanese *onsen* have several unique aspects that distinguish them from their counterparts in other countries.

Task 10-4 ➤ Outlining

Topic sentence をサポートするポイントを箇条書きにした outline を書きましょう。

Example

1. originated as *"toji"*
   treat illness / long history /
   composition of water / effectiveness
2. etiquette
   naked / cleaning the body / no towels in water / → clean water
   no swimming or playing → quiet relaxation
3. *onsen* + spa hotels
   distinctive robes / traditional cuisine / sleep on floor
   → truly unique

Task 10-5 ➤

この他に自分の好きな日本の文化・風習を説明するセンテンスを書いてみましょう。

Task 10-6 ➤ Writing Supporting Sentences

Task 10-4 でたてたポイントのひとつひとつを、それぞれ２つ以上のセンテンスで表現してください。比較しているそれぞれの特徴をそれぞれ触れるようにします。

Example

1. originated as *"toji"*
   treat illness / long history /
   composition of water / effectiveness

· **Japanese *onsen* originated as places for "hot spring cures" to treat illness and restore health**. *Onsen* as places to recover and improve health appears in ancient books. Even today, each *onsen* provides detailed information about the composition of its hot water and claims its effectiveness.

2. etiquette

   naked / cleaning the body / no towels in water / → clean water

   no swimming or playing → quiet relaxation

   · **Japanese *onsen* have unique bathing manners and etiquette**. For example, bathing naked without a bathing suit, cleaning the body before entering the tub and not putting towels in the tub are all meant to keep the water clean. Swimming and playing in the water are not acceptable in the baths, as they are considered places for quiet relaxation.

3. *onsen* + spa hotels

   distinctive robes / traditional cuisine / sleep on the floor

   → truly unique

   · **Japanese *onsen* are packaged with traditional spa hotels or *ryokan***. At a *ryokan*, in addition to soaking in an *onsen*, you can enjoy wearing distinctive robes, eating traditional cuisine and sleeping on the floor, which is truly unique.

Task 10-7 ► Writing Concluding Sentences

Unit 4 で学んだ３つのテクニークで、concluding sentence を書いてみましょう。

1）**Example**

Technique 1 (Restating the topic sentence):

In this way, Japanese *onsen* have characteristics that are not found in hot springs in other countries.

Technique 2 (Summarizing the main points):

To summarize, Japanese *onsen* are special in that they are a total experience, combining bathing as a therapy, unique bathing customs and traditional accommodations.

Technique 3 (Giving a final thought):

I hope that as many foreigners as possible will experience this Japanese hot spring culture.

いままで書いた文を改めてパラグラフにまとめましょう。構成を明確にするためのつなぎ言葉も使いましょう。また、文のパタンが単調にならないよう、センテンスの始まりに変化をつけましょう。

Example

Enjoy the Unique Characteristics of Japanese *Onsen*

In recent years, the number of foreign tourists visiting Japan has increased. Each of them may have their own particular taste that they are looking for. One of the most popular aspects of Japanese culture among foreigners is *onsen* (hot springs). **Japanese *onsen* have several unique aspects that distinguish them from their counterparts in other countries.** Firstly, **Japanese *onsen* originated as places for "hot spring cures" to treat illness and restore health.** *Onsen* as a place to recover and improve health appears in ancient books. Today, each *onsen* provides detailed information about the chemical composition of its hot water and claims its effectiveness. Secondly, Japanese *onsen* have unique **bathing manners and etiquette, such as** bathing naked without a bathing suit, cleaning the body before entering the tub and not putting towels in the tub. These are all meant to keep the water clean. Swimming and playing in the water are not allowed in the baths, as they are considered places for quiet relaxation. **Finally, Japanese onsen are packaged with traditional *ryokan* (spa hotels).** At a *ryokan*, in addition to soaking in an *onsen*, you can enjoy wearing distinctive robes, eating traditional cuisine and sleeping on the floor, which is truly unique. In this way, Japanese *onsen* are special in that they are a total experience, combining bathing as a therapy, unique bathing customs and traditional accommodations. We hope that as many foreigners as possible will experience this Japanese hot spring culture. Soaking naked in hot water with complete strangers is an experience that cannot be had anywhere else.

▐▌ Focusing on Form

Choppiness (II)

Unit 9 に引き続き、choppiness を直す練習です。

Now *you* try *!*

1～5 それぞれに含まれるすべての情報を、それぞれ 1 センテンスで表現してみましょう。

1. *Hanami* is a Japanese annual event. *Hanami* literally means blossom viewing. In this event, people hold wild parties. They do so under cherry blossom trees.

   _____

   _____

   _____

2. The College Festival is held in autumn every year. It is an important occasion for students. The members of our club spend a long time preparing for it.

   _____

   _____

   _____

3. I think that you should stay off your phone for some time. You should do so for two hours, at the very least. That is before you go to bed. I have three reasons. The reasons are the following.

   _____

   _____

   _____

4. I argue that smoking should be banned in all public places. I argue so for several reasons. The most important reason is this. Secondhand smoke affects the health of others.

_____

_____

_____

5. People in the West have a stereotype about the Japanese. The stereotype is that the Japanese are a diligent nation. It is also that they are difficult to understand. This movie reinforces that stereotype.

_____

_____

_____

Narrating Past Events

忘れられない、あの出来事

このユニットでは印象に残った出来事（楽しかったこと、つらかったこと、など）を書いてみましょう。

まずは次の例をみてください。「ゼミで日帰りスキー・スノボ旅行に行った」という経験について書くために、まず質問に答えていきます。

Example

1. **What is the unforgettable event that you are going to describe?**
   — Going skiing and snowboarding with my seminar group.

2. **Any additional information on the event?**
   — It is an annual event of our seminar.

3. **In what way was the event unforgettable? Choose two or three adjectives that fit from below:**

fun	educational	challenging
enjoyable	informative	painful
amusing	insightful	tough
hilarious	inspirational	sad
pleasurable	enriching	disappointing
thrilling	empowering	regrettable
exciting	life-changing	insulting
intense	meaningful	resentful
entertaining	rewarding	frustrating
energetic	engaging	infuriating

   — It was fun and exciting.

4. **When and for how long did the event take place?**
   — At the end of January, right after the autumn term ended. It was a one-day event.

5. **Who else "took part" in this event?**
   — My seminar professor and eight students in the seminar.

6. **Where did that event take place?**
   — Gala Yuzawa Ski Resort in Niigata Prefecture.

7. **Any additional information about that place?**
   — It is located 90 minutes from Tokyo by Shinkansen (bullet train).
   — It is promoted as a "come empty-handed and ski" ski resort with a full range of rental equipment.
   — The Shinkansen ticket gate is directly connected to the resort's reception and rental desks.

8. **What happened first?**
   — My seminar professor and eight of us students met at Tokyo Station, boarded the 7:36 Shinkansen and got off at Gala Yuzawa around 9:00.

9. **What happened then?**
   — We got our gondola/lift tickets and rental equipment, changed, got on the gondolas and were ready to hit the slopes at 9:40.

10. **What happened then?**
    — We split into three groups according to ability and started skiing or snowboarding.

11. **What happened next?**
    — We skied or snowboarded for about six hours on and off, with lunch and coffee breaks in between, until 4pm, when it started to get dark.

12. **Any other details to add?**
    — The snow was good and the weather was perfect.
    — The professor and two students were skiing, while the other six were snowboarding.
    — It was my first time snowboarding.

13. **Describe your feeling(s) at one or more points during the event.**
    — It was scary to get both feet on the board because I could not move them separately like I do when skiing.
    — I felt good when I managed to go down the slope for the first time without falling.
    — The new feeling of going down the slope on a snowboard was thrilling.
    — I felt that the bonds between the professor and us students and between us students was strengthened.

14. **How would you sum up the experience?**
    — It was an intense experience packed into a short day.
    — It was a great break from the academic activities during the semester.

以上の回答をつなぎ合わせ、内容のまとまりごとにパラグラフにし、短いエッセイを作りました。複数の回答をひとつのセンテンスにまとめたり、つながりを良くするために順番を調整したり、繰り返しを避けるために表現を変えたりしています。上の回答と異なる部分に下線を引いてチェックしましょう。

🔊 **Audio 24**

One of my most fun and exciting recent events was going skiing and snowboarding with my seminar group, which is an annual event of the seminar. It took place at the end of January, right after the autumn term ended.

The professor and eight students in the seminar went to Gala Yuzawa Ski Resort in Niigata Prefecture. Gala is located 90 minutes from Tokyo by Shinkansen, and is promoted as a "come empty-handed and ski" ski resort with a full range of rental equipment.

Nine of us met at Tokyo Station, boarded the 7:36 Shinkansen and got off at Gala Yuzawa around 9:00. The Shinkansen ticket gate is directly connected to the resort's reception and rental desks, so it takes no time to get ready. We got our gondola/lift tickets and rental equipment, changed, got on the gondolas and were ready to hit the slopes by 9:40.

The snow was good and the weather was perfect. The professor and two students were skiing, while the other six, including myself, were snowboarding. We split into three groups according to ability and started skiing or snowboarding. It was my first time snowboarding. I was scared at first to get both my feet on the board because I could not move them separately like I do when skiing. But my friends taught me step by step and after a while, I felt good when I managed to go down the slope for the first time without falling. I was thrilled with the new feeling of going down the slope on a snowboard.

We skied and snowboarded for about six hours on and off, with lunch and coffee breaks in between, until 4pm, when it started to get dark. I felt that the bonds between the professor and us students and between us students was strengthened. We were back in Tokyo by 6pm. It was an intense experience packed into a short day and a great break from the academic activities during the semester.

Task 11-1

上の例にならって、何らかの出来ごと、体験について書いてみましょう。まず質問に1文ないし2文程度の答えを書いてみましょう。

1. What is the unforgettable event that you are going to describe?

_____

_____

2. Any additional information on the event?

_____

_____

3. In what way was the event unforgettable? Choose two or three adjectives that fit from below:

fun	educational	challenging
enjoyable	informative	painful
amusing	insightful	tough
hilarious	inspirational	sad
pleasurable	enriching	disappointing
thrilling	empowering	regrettable
exciting	life-changing	insulting
intense	meaningful	resentful
entertaining	rewarding	frustrating
energetic	engaging	infuriating

_____

_____

4. When and for how long did the event take place?

_____

_____

5. Who else "took part" in this event?

_____

_____

6. Where did that event take place?

_____

7. Any additional information about that place?

_____

_____

8. What happened first?

_____

_____

9. What happened then?

_____

_____

10. What happened then?

_____

_____

11. What happened next?

_____

_____

12. Any other details to add?

_____

_____

13. Describe your feeling(s) at one or more points during the event.

_____

_____

_____

_____

14. How would you sum up the experience?

_____

_____

Task 11-2 ▶

Task 11-1 の回答をつなぎ合わせ、内容のまとまりごとにパラグラフにし、短いエッセイ を作ってみましょう。複数の回答をひとつのセンテンスにまとめたり、つながりを良くす るために順番を調整したり、繰り返しを避けるために表現を変えたりもしてみましょう。

📖 Focusing on Form

Parallel Structure

(both) A and B / (either) A or B / A, B, and C / A, B, or C などの構造において、A と B（および C）は、同等の文法構造をもつ（parallel である）必要があります。

Now *you* try❗

例にならって、parallel でない部分を parallel に直しましょう。

Example: Anna is honest, kind, and has a warm heart.
　　　　　→ Anna is honest, kind, and warm-hearted.

1. The most important when I make a decision is to choose what I love and interesting.

　　_____

　　_____

2. Two things that are particularly important to me are playing baseball and I like reading.

　　_____

　　_____

3. I really enjoy both skiing and the flute.

　　_____

　　_____

4. Whereas most married couples use the husband's family name, the wife's name is used in some cases.

　　_____

　　_____

5. At our university there are approximately 600 teachers and it has a clerical staff of 400.

_____

_____

6. Scientists now know how the disease is spread and about its prevention.

_____

_____

7. Their music is so cool, wild, and moves me.

_____

_____

Describing Data Expressed in Graphs
データにみる世界の現状

この Unit では、図や表から情報を読み取ってパラグラフを書く練習をしましょう。

国政の場でどの程度女性が活躍しているかは、国によってかなり違いがあるようです。図1（Figure 1）から情報を読み取り、質問に full sentence で答えると次のようになります。

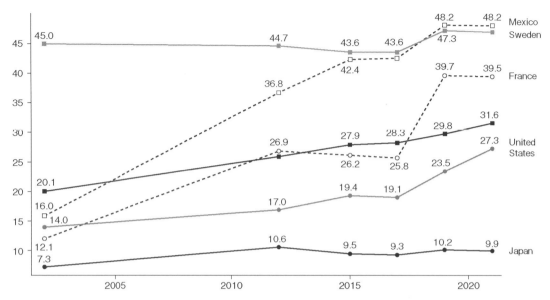

Figure 1. Percentages of Women Parliamentarians in Five OECD Countries (2001-2021) (source: https://www.oecd.org/coronavirus/en/data-insights/women-in-parliament-reached-31-6percent-in-2021)

Example

1. **What does Figure 1 show?**
   — Figure 1 shows the percentage of women in national parliaments in five countries and the OECD average from 2001 to 2021.

2. **Which five countries are they?**
   — The five countries are Mexico, Sweden, France, the United States and Japan.

3. **What was the OECD average in 2001, and what was it in 2021?**
   — The OECD average was 20.1% in 2001, rising steadily to 31.6% in 2021.

4. **Does how the figures have changed over time vary from country to country?**
   How the figures have changed over the years varies considerably from country to country.

5. **Of the five countries, by which country was the largest increase of what points achieved, from what percentage in 2001 to what percentage in 2021?**

— Of the five countries, the largest increase of 32.2 points was achieved by Mexico, from 16% in 2001 to 48.2% in 2021.

6. **In which country is the second largest increase of what points seen, from what percent in 2001 to what percent in 2021?**
   — The second largest increase of 27.4 points is seen in France, from 12.1% in 2001 to 39.5% in 2021.

7. **What can be said about Sweden?**
   — Sweden's share hasn't changed much; it was already quite high at 45% in 2001 and is now slightly higher at 47%.

8. **What about Japan?**
   — In Japan, the proportion of women in parliament has remained low, rising only slightly from 7.3% in 2002 to 9.9% in 2021.

9. **How can you summarize the data?**
   — Although there is still a long way to go to achieve gender parity, the overall situation is improving. But Japan seems to be lagging far behind the other countries.

以上の回答をつなぎ合わせてパラグラフを作りました。センテンス間のつながりをよりなめらかにするためにつなぎ言葉を使ったり、繰り返しを避けるために表現を変えたり、補ったりしています。上の回答と異なる部分に下線を引いてチェックしましょう。

🔊 **Audio 25**

Figure 1 shows the percentage of women in national parliaments in five countries and the OECD average from 2001 to 2021. The five countries are Mexico, Sweden, France, the United States and Japan. The OECD average was 20.1% in 2001, rising steadily to 31.6% in 2021. However, how the figures have changed over the years varies considerably from country to country. Of the five countries, the largest increase of 32.2 points was achieved by Mexico, from 16% in 2001 to 48.2% in 2021. The second largest increase is seen in France, where the figure rises by 27.4 points from 12.1% to 39.5%. Sweden's share hasn't changed much; it was already quite high at 45% in 2001 and is now slightly higher at 47%. In Japan, on the other hand, the proportion of women in parliament has remained low, rising only slightly from 7.3% in 2002 to 9.9% in 2021. In summary, although there is still a long way to go to achieve gender parity, the overall situation is improving. However, Japan seems to be lagging far behind the other countries.

Task 12-1

世界の人口は増加が続いており 2050 年には 97 億人に達すると見込まれています。1950年から 2021 年までの人口の変化について Table 1 と Figure 2 から読み取れる情報について下の質問に答えましょう。

Country or region	1950	2021	Absolute Change	Relative Change
China	543,979,200	1,425,893,500	+881,914,300	+162%
India	357,021,120	1,407,563,900	+1,050,542,780	+294%
United States	148,281,550	336,997,630	+188,716,080	+127%
Indonesia	69,567,624	273,753,180	+204,185,556	+294%
Pakistan	37,696,264	231,402,110	+193,705,846	+514%

Table 1. Population change 1950-2021 in the 5 most populous countries
(Source: https://ourworldindata.org/explorers/population-and-demography?tab=table&
facet=none&country=CHN~IND~USA~IDN~PAK&hideControls=false&Metric=Population
&Sex=Both+sexes&Age+group=Total&Projection+Scenario=None)

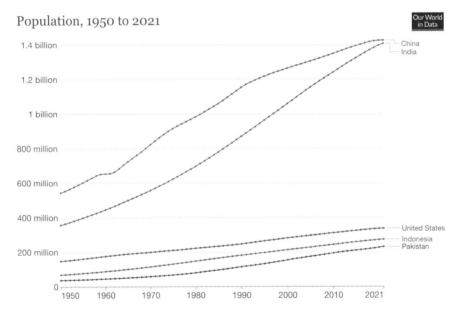

Figure 2. Population change 1950-2021 in the 5 most populous countries
(Source: United Nations, World Population Prospects, 2022)

1. What does Table 1 show?

_____

_____

_____

2. How does Figure 2 show the same information as Table 1?

_____

_____

_____

3. What were the five most populous countries in 2021?

_____

_____

_____

4. What is the difference in population between China and India in 2021? Is it relatively large or small compared to their total populations?

_____

_____

_____

5. What are the relative changes for India and China and how do they compare?

_____

_____

_____

6. Based on the answers to 5, what is likely to happen?

_____

_____

_____

7. Can this prediction be confirmed graphically by the lines for the two countries in Figure 2?

_____

_____

_____

8. Which country, apart from China and India, has seen the greatest absolute change? How much has its population increased over these 71 years?

_____

_____

_____

9. Which country has experienced the greatest relative change and by what percentage? That is, how many times larger was its population in 2021 than it was in 1950?

_____

_____

_____

10. How can you summarize the data?

_____

_____

_____

Task 12-2

🎧 Audio 26

Task 12-1 の 1 ～ 11 に対する答えをもとにパラグラフを書きましょう。センテンス間の つながりをよくするためにつなぎ言葉を使ったり、繰り返しを避けるために表現を変えた りすることに気をつけてください。解答例は音声を聞いて確認しましょう。

地球温暖化の影響で北極の氷の面積はどのように変化しているでしょうか。Figure 3 から情報を読み取り、下の質問に full sentence で答えましょう。

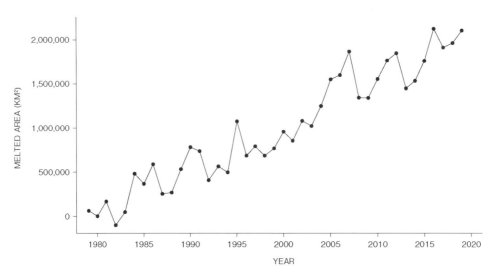

Figure 3. Sea ice loss in the arctic ocean
(Source: https://earth.org/data_visualization/the-effect-of-sea-ice-decline-on-polar-bear-habitats/)

1. What does Figure 3 show?

_____

_____

2. From what year to what year were the measurements taken?

_____

_____

3. What does the vertical axis show?

_____

_____

4. Where is the origin of the vertical axis set?

_____

_____

5. What does the horizontal axis show?

_____

_____

6. How did the area that melted from 1981 to 2019 compare with the area that melted in 1980? Are there any exceptions?

_____

_____

7. What is the the overall trend from decade to decade? Is the trend clear? Have there been any fluctuations?

_____

_____

8. How much was the area lost in 1990, 2000, 2010, and 2019?

_____

_____

9. How can you summarize the data?

_____

_____

Task 12-3 で書いたセンテンスをまとめてパラグラフにしてみましょう。その際、つなぎ言葉を使ったり、繰り返しを避けるために表現を変えたりすることに気をつけましょう。解答例は音声を聞いて確認しましょう。

地球温暖化を遅らせるためには二酸化炭素排出量の削減が急務と言われています。国別の状況を表す Figure 4 についての 1 〜 11 の質問に full sentence で答えましょう。

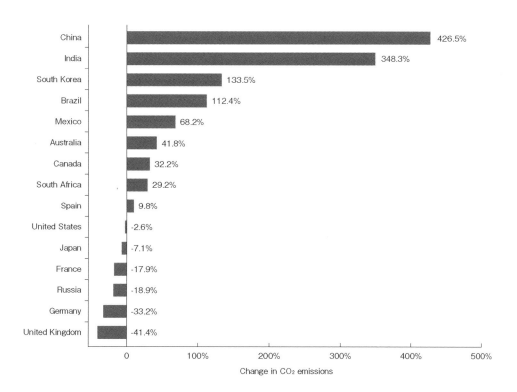

Figure 4. Percentage change in CO2 emissions in selected countries from 1990 to 2021 (Source: https://www.statista.com/statistics/270500/percentage-change-in-co2-emissions-in-selected-countries/)

1. What does Figure 4 show?

_____

_____

2. What does the vertical axis show?

_____

3. What does the horizontal axis show?

_____

_____

4. What exactly does the figure for each country mean?

_____

_____

5. How many countries have higher CO2 emissions in 2021 than in 1990 and how many lower?

_____

_____

6. How many countries emit more than 300% more CO2 in 2021 than in 1990?

_____

_____

7. What are their exact percentages?

_____

_____

8. Are the percentages for South Korea and Brazil above 100? What does that mean?

_____

_____

9. In which country was the largest negative percentage change recorded? What percentage lower was the value than in 1990?

_____

_____

10. In which country was the second largest negative percentage change? What percentage lower was the value than in 1990?

_____

_____

11. How can you summarize the data?

_____

_____

Task 12-6 ◄ 𝔞 Audio 28

Task 12-5 で書いたセンテンスをまとめてパラグラフにしてみましょう。その際、つなぎ言葉を使ったり、繰り返しを避けるために表現を変えたりすることに気をつけましょう。解答例は音声を聞いて確認しましょう。

```



```

毎年世界で製造される４億トンのプラスチックの中で、一度使用したら廃棄される single-use plastic は、約 47% にも上り、それらの 79% が埋め立てられ、もしくは海洋等に投棄されているとされます。地球環境を守るためにはそのような single-use plastic を減らすことが急務です。国別の状況を Figure 5 から読み取り、パラグラフにまとめてみましょう。

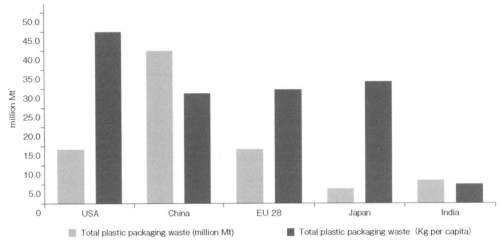

Figure 5. Plastic packaging waste generation, 2014 (Source: Adapted from Geyer, Jambeck, and Law, 2017)

Appendix: Additional Cues for Writing

People
1. What are the qualities of good parents?
2. Describe your appearance. What do you like most about the way you look? What features do you want to change?
3. Take two members of your family or two friends, and compare them. What are some of the differences and the similarities?
4. When you have a problem, whose advice do you seek most often, and why?
5. Do you agree or disagree with the following statement? "A man and a woman can never be friends." Give specific reasons and examples to support your answer.
6. Do you agree or disagree with the following statement? The first impression of a person is sometimes very different from who they really are. Give specific reasons and examples to support your answer.

Food
7. If you knew that the world were coming to an end (for whatever reason) today, what would you like to eat for your last meal?
8. What is your favorite dish? Explain what it is like and how to prepare it assuming the reader is a non-Japanese person.
9. Which do you prefer, dining at restaurants or having dinner at home? Give specific reasons and examples to support your answer.
10. Nowadays, many more types of ready-made foods are available at supermarkets and convenience stores than before. Has this change improved the way people live? Give specific reasons and examples to support your answer.

Places
11. What is your favorite place to spend a one-day holiday?
12. A person you know is planning to move to your town or city. What do you think this person would like and dislike about living in your town or city? Why?
13. Describe your favorite restaurant. What are the food, the service, and the decor like?

14. Which do you think is better, living in a big city or in a small town? Give specific reasons and details to support your answer.

Sports and Entertainment
15. What are some sports that you would like to try some day?
16. What are some of the sports that you would never want to try?
17. Describe a good movie that you watched recently. What did you like about it?
18. Some people prefer Japanese songs to English songs. Other people prefer English songs to Japanese songs. Which type are you?
19. People have different ways of getting rid of stress. Some read; some exercise; others play computer games. What is your favorite way? Give specific details and examples in your answer.
20. When you watch a movie, do you prefer to watch it in a movie theater or at home as an on-demand video?
21. Do you agree or disagree with the following statement? Movies and TV programs substantially affect how people behave. Give specific reasons and examples to support your answer.
22. Do you agree or disagree with the following statement? TV programs are spending too much time covering the personal lives of celebrities. Give specific reasons and examples to support your answer.
23. Do you agree or disagree with the following statement? Generally speaking, foreign movies are more interesting than Japanese movies. Give specific reasons and examples to support your answer.

Lifestyle
24. What do you do every day? Describe your typical day. What do you do think about your daily schedule?
25. What do you like to do in your free time?
26. Some people prefer to get up early in the morning and start the days work. Others prefer to get up later in the day and work until late at night. Which do you prefer? Use specific reasons and examples to support your choice.
27. Some people prefer to spend most of their time alone. Others like to be with friends most of the time. Which type are you? Give specific reasons to support your answer.

28. In the next twenty years, what changes do you think will take place in society?
29. What imaginary invention would you like to have to improve your life?
30. In your opinion, what was the greatest invention in human history?
31. What does the following proverb mean? A rolling stone gathers no moss. Do you agree or disagree with the idea?
32. What does the following proverb mean? Every cloud has a silver lining. What do you think of the idea expressed in it?
33. Do you agree or disagree with the following statement? Telling a lie is sometimes a good thing. Give specific reasons and examples to support your answer.

School and Education
34. What are the qualities of a good university?
35. What are the qualities of a good university student?
36. What are the qualities of a good university teacher?
37. If you were to cite three good points of your university, what would they be?
38. If you were to cite three bad points of your university, what would they be?
39. There are classes in which the teacher does most of the talking, as well as those where students discuss various issues. Which type of class do you prefer?
40. When an examination is drawing near, do you prefer to study alone or together with your friends?
41. Do you agree or disagree with the following statement? If there were no examinations or required papers, students would not study as much. Give specific reasons and examples to support your answer.
42. Do you agree or disagree with the following statement? Whether a student comes to like or dislike a certain school subject depends a lot on who is teaching it. Give specific reasons and examples to support your answer.
43. Do you agree or disagree with the following statement? Being a university student is tough. Give specific reasons and examples to support your answer.
44. Do you agree or disagree with the following statement? Universities should ask students to evaluate their teachers. Give specific reasons and examples to support your answer.
45. Do you agree or disagree with the following statement? High schools

should ask students to evaluate their teachers. Give specific reasons and examples to support your answer.

46. Do you agree or disagree with the following statement? Primary schools should ask pupils to evaluate their teachers. Give specific reasons and examples to support your answer.

47. Do you agree or disagree with the following statement? Universities should admit anyone willing to study, without any screening. Give specific reasons and examples to support your answer.

48. Do you agree or disagree with the following statement? When learning something, it is always better to have a teacher. Give specific reasons and examples to support your answer.

49. If your university had an extra budget of ten million yen, what do you think would be the best way to spend it? Give specific reasons and details to support your choice.

50. Recall your high school and the days you spent there. If you could make one important change in the high school that you attended, what change would you make? Give reasons and specific examples to support your answer.

51. Some children spend a great amount of their time going to and studying at cram schools. Discuss the advantages and disadvantages of this. Use specific reasons and examples to support your answer.

Job

52. When choosing a job in the future, what points will be important to you? The pay level, flexibility of working time, creativity involved in the job, prestige associated with it, or something else?

53. Would you prefer joining and working for a large corporation or starting your own business?

54. Do you agree or disagree with the following statement? Everyone should retire at the age of 50 to give their position to a younger person. Give specific reasons and examples to support your position.

Animals and the Environment

55. Some people treat pets as members of their family. Do you think such a relationship between humans and animals is a good one?

56. Do you agree or disagree with the following statement? It is wrong and disrespectful to keep animals in zoos. Give specific reasons and examples to support your answer.

57. Do you agree or disagree with the following statement? It is morally wrong to use animals in experiments to test the safety of such non-essential products as cosmetics. Give specific reasons and examples to support your answer.

58. Do you agree or disagree with the following statement? Human needs for development are more important than saving land for endangered animals. Give specific reasons and examples to support your answer.

59. Pets' lives are generally shorter than their owners'. Some people might want to have clones of their pets so that they can be accompanied by their loved ones all through their lives. Do you think this is acceptable?

Social Issues

60. In Japan, people are no longer allowed to smoke in many public places and office buildings. Do you think this is a good rule or a bad rule? Use specific reasons and details to support your position.

61. It has recently been announced that a new convenience store may be built right in front of your apartment (or house). Do you support or oppose this plan? Why? Use specific reasons and details to support your answer.

62. Even today, women are not allowed to step on a sumo-wrestling dohyo. Do you think this is a form of sexual discrimination that should be condemned or a tradition to be kept?

63. It is very common to see hundreds of bicycles left in front of, or near, railway stations. They block most of the sidewalks, so people have a hard time walking by. What are some solutions to this problem?

64. The population of Japan is slowly decreasing. What are the causes of this phenomenon, and what will be some consequences?

65. Today, Coming-of-Age-Day ceremonies are not what they used to be. There are countless reports of young participants disrupting the ceremonies by chatting, drinking, and even setting off fireworks during the speeches. What are some causes of this phenomenon and what are some solutions?

66. Today the legal age for drinking is twenty, but most university first-year

students have opportunities to drink semi-legally. Do you think the legal age for drinking should be lowered?

67. Under the current system in Japan, married couples are required to use the same family name. Some people insist that the law should be revised so that married couples can retain two different family names if they wish to do so. What is your position on this issue?

Writing Accelerator
パラグラフ構成要素から学べるライティング入門

2024 年 4 月 10 日　初版第 1 刷発行

著　者　靜　哲人

発行者　森　信久
発行所　**株式会社　松柏社**
〒 102-0072　東京都千代田区飯田橋 1-6-1
TEL　03 (3230) 4813 （代表）
FAX　03 (3230) 4857
http://www.shohakusha.com
e-mail: info@shohakusha.com

装　　幀　小島トシノブ（NONdesign）
印刷・製本　中央精版印刷株式会社

略号＝ 790

ISBN978-4-88198-790-2